out of BOUNDS

scrapbooking *without* boundaries

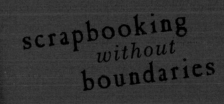

jodi amidei
and
torrey scott

 Memory Makers Books
Cincinnati, Ohio
www.memorymakersmagazine.com

11 10 09 08 07 5 4 3 2 1

Distributed in Canada by Fraser Direct
100 Armstrong Avenue
Georgetown, ON, Canada L7G 5S4
Tel: (905) 877-4411

Distributed in the U.K. and Europe by David & Charles
Brunel House, Newton Abbot, Devon, TQ12 4PU, England
Tel: (+44) 1626 323200, Fax: (+44) 1626 323319
Email: postmaster@davidandcharles.co.uk

Distributed in Australia by Capricorn Link
P.O. Box 704, S. Windsor NSW, 2756 Australia
Tel: (02) 4577-3555

Library of Congress Cataloging-in-Publication Data
Amidei, Jodi
    Out of bounds : scrapbooking without boundaries / Jodi Amidei and Torrey Scott.
        p. cm.
    Includes index.
    ISBN-13: 978-1-59963-009-0 (softcover : alk. paper)
    ISBN-10: 1-59963-009-5 (softcover : alk. paper)
    1. Scrapbooks. I. Scott, Torrey II. Title.
TR501.A4857 2007
745.593--dc22
                            2007000515

Editor: Amy Glander
Cover Designers: Amanda Dalton and Jeremy Werling
Interior Designer: Jeremy Werling
Art Coordinator: Eileen Aber
Production Coordinator: Matt Wagner
Photographers: Robert Best and Kris Kandler
Adam Leigh-Manuell and John Carrico, Alias Imaging, LLC
Stylist: Jan Nickum

fw

F+W PUBLICATIONS, INC.

Our lives are filled with inspiration in everything we see and do. We have been given wings to fly by all those who have touched our lives and our souls, and for this we are truly grateful. We are also continually thankful that neither of us had to be fitted for a straightjacket during the process of creating this book.

TABLE OF CONTENTS

6   **Introduction**

8   CHAPTER ONE
Playing With Techniques

38   CHAPTER TWO
There Are No Rules

66   CHAPTER THREE
The Motivation Behind

94   CHAPTER FOUR
Outside the Album

120   **Author Tribute**

124   **Source Guide**

127   **Index**

CHAPTER ONE | **PLAYING WITH TECHNIQUES**

CHAPTER TWO | **THERE ARE NO RULES**

CHAPTER THREE | **THE MOTIVATION BEHIND**

CHAPTER FOUR | **OUTSIDE THE ALBUM**

JoJo Mojo

Photo: Kelli Noto

Our world today is saturated with rules, regulations and guidelines. These expectations overshadow not only our work, but also loom over almost every aspect of our daily lives. It seems that nothing is immune to this regimentation—not even our creative outlets. This, unfortunately, includes our passion for scrapbooking.

Through years of teaching and working with scrapbookers all over the world, we have found that many are not only craving to break free, but are also finally ready to release themselves from the hold of these self-imposed rules and start enjoying their passion again. We are continually looking for ways to expand and change our perspectives and conceptions about why we choose this craft as our creative outlet. For scrapbookers, scrapbooking is what keeps many of us sane. So it's absolutely vital that we foster and nurture our creative spirit.

Within the following pages, together we will explore unrivaled and innovative techniques, toss the rules of design out the window, open the door of provocative motivations behind why we scrapbook, and finally set our creativity free from the album itself.

Let us share with you the vision of what we've discovered—that there really are no rules in scrapbooking. It is whatever you want it to be. It's time we give ourselves permission to let go of the boundaries and allow the creative synergy to soar. After all, scrapbooking, like life, is a journey, not a destination. So put on your creativity shoes (or go barefoot) and join us on the road to rediscovering our love of this wonderful craft.

Jodi Torrey

Playing With Techniques

Scrapbook pages with out-of-the-box techniques

Techniques. It's such an intimidating term for something that is truly the most fun part of scrapbooking. When we talk about techniques, all we are really talking about is having fun exploring and experimenting with different products to see what they can do—and what they can't do. It's all about discovery and creating with fearless abandon. It's also about allowing ourselves to make "mistakes." But actually, there are no mistakes here…only "flopportunities"—opportunities to employ our creativity. By allowing ourselves to just go with the flow and play, we will most likely be pleasantly surprised with the results. Sometimes these "happy accidents" will find their place in our technique cache amongst our favorites. The best way to learn techniques is to play with them. So let's fire up the laboratory and start 'sperimenting. It's time to let loose that creative muse.

CHAPTER ONE

Carousel

Ever since I was a girl, I've loved carousels... and I still do. Whether it's a herd of prancing horses, or an entire zoo on parade ... carousels are the best!

Wood-Burning Tool

While recently watching a movie about summer camp, I was instantly transported back to those carefree days of Popsicle stick birdhouses, God's Eyes made of yarn and twigs and, most of all, the scent of burning wood from blazing campfires. And then I remembered, "Hey! I have a wood-burning tool upstairs." This revelation "sparked" my wood-burned page. A quick trip to the hardware store provided me with all the materials I needed for the layout. The rest I accomplished with a little creativity and my handy wood-burning tool. From the decorative elements and designs to the title and journaling, everything on this layout is burned into the wood. Everything except the photos, that is.

Today, wood-burning tools come with interchangeable tips to allow you creative freedom in your designs. It produces a really good aroma, too (if you like the smell of campfires). To protect your precious photos, seal the whole shebang with acrylic sealant before you adhere them to the layout.

Artist: Torrey

Supplies: Wood-burning tool (Walnut Hollow); decorative stencil (Dèjá Views); decorative wood shapes, molding, plywood (Home Depot); acrylic paint (Delta, Plaid); acrylic sealant (Krylon)

If you can dream it, you can do it.
– Walt Disney

Hardware Store, Here I Come

Take a trip to your local hardware store, but this time do so with an artful eye. Look at things with regard to their shape and form instead of their intended purpose. My favorite departments? The paint chip displays, electrical supply section and the hardware section. There are treasures everywhere. All it takes is some out-of-the-box thinking.

PHOTO OP

ok, I admit it... I see the world through a scrapbookers eyes - everything I see is inspiration for a page, some journaling or a new photo opportunity. Take this wall for instance, as soon as I saw it I knew it would make a great backdrop for a photo shoot. Good thing Haley is such a good sport and willing to indulge me with yet another photo op.

Rolled Paper Collage

While glancing through a fine art book at a local bookstore, I came across a rolled paper collage that caught my eye. I knew then and there I had to try it on a layout—and I promise, it's not as hard as it looks.

Start by creating the framework boxes using painted chipboard pieces glued into the desired designs. Using a small dowel rod as a guide, roll 2" (5cm) patterned paper squares into tightly wound rolls. Then, fill each frame section with rolls of different sizes and colors. A coating of crystal lacquer finishes and seals it.

Here you see how this technique works as a unique and colorful border, but you can also accomplish the same look on a smaller scale. You may want to add some detail or a burst of color to a tag, title or small page accent. Don't be afraid to experiment—in the end you'll love the results.

Artist: Jodi

Supplies: Patterned paper (Adorn It, Heidi Grace, Karen Foster, Magenta, Provo Craft, PSX); textured cardstock (Die Cuts With A View, Prism); acrylic paint (Delta); crystal lacquer (Sakura)

> The best way to have a good idea is to have lots of ideas.
> – Linus Pauling

Artist Challenge

The next time you are browsing through your favorite bookstore, stop in the fine art section and peruse some books. Take a notebook and jot down three inspiring ideas that could translate into scrapbooking.

It's not easy, but once you get Kyli to smile she lights up the room. She's slow to trust, but when you gain her confidence you realize it's been well worth the effort. She is the daughter of a dear friend and it's been such a pleasure to get to know her better.

kyli

Watercolor Paints & Stamping

Scrapbooking has given me reason to dabble in many art forms. I'm definitely not an experienced watercolor artist, but this simple background was a cinch to create using a piece of watercolor paper for the background. All it took was a 1" (2.54cm) straight-edged brush, an inexpensive set of watercolor paints and a steady hand.

The simple black stamps sparkle and shine through the rainbow of color. The elements were so striking that the page was almost done without adding anything else. A few extra stamped flowers, silhouette-cut and popping off the page, was all it took to finish off this kaleidoscope of color.

Artist: Jodi

Supplies: Textured cardstock (Paper Studio); watercolor paper (Big Art Brand); watercolor paints (Canson); letter stamps (Technique Tuesday); stamps (Hero Arts, Plaid, Scrappy Cat, Stamps by Judith); chalk ink (Clearsnap); stamping ink (Tsukineko); photo corners (Junkitz); brads (Creative Impressions); glitter glue (Ranger); glitter pen (Sakura)

The world is but a canvas to the imagination.
– Henry David Thoreau

Try Watercolors

This technique is so simple; you've got to give it a try. You can even try this technique on regular cardstock—just limit the amount of water you use, and when allowing it to dry, press it under a heavy book to ensure it will lie flat without curling the edges.

Favorite Asian **PROVERBS**

If you wish to know the mind of a man, listen to his words.

When the character of a man is not clear to you, look at his friends.

Laws control the lesser man. Right conduct controls the greater one.

To teach is to learn.

A bad word whispered will echo a hundred miles.

If you are patient in one moment of anger, you will escape a hundred days of sorrow.

Deal with the faults of others as gently as with your own.

A clever person turns great troubles into little ones and little ones into none at all.

Better to light a candle than to curse the darkness.

Small men think they are small; great men never know they are great.

Heaven lent you a soul. Earth will lend a grave.

The tongue is more to be feared than the sword.

One generation plants the trees; another gets the shade.

He who asks is a fool for five minutes, but he who does not ask remains a fool forever.

A thorn defends the rose, harming only those who would steal the blossom.

A wise man makes his own decisions; an ignorant man follows the public opinion.

There are many paths to the top of the mountain, but the view is always the same.

A rumor goes in one ear and out many mouths.

Mankind fears an evil man but heaven does not.

Photos Printed on Woven Paper

The Chinese philosopher Confucius said, "Perseverance is a virtue." Well, I don't know if Confucius really said that, but I've found it to be true—especially in my scrapbooking.

This woven bamboo plant always fascinated me. So when I decided to do a layout about my favorite Asian proverbs, I knew I wanted to use a photo of it. But that wasn't enough. I wanted to mimic the weaving in my design, as well. Enter lightweight, handmade rice paper. I started with strips of different widths and wove them tightly into a striking surface for the photo.

I'll admit my first attempt didn't produce the look I was going for. I tried feeding the woven paper through my printer to print the photo directly on the surface. Let's just say that didn't work out as planned. But I knew it was still the look I wanted, so I improvised and came up with another idea. I printed the photo onto an iron-on transfer sheet and transferred it directly onto the woven rice paper. The end result was exactly what I was going for. It was well worth learning one way it wouldn't work to discover one way it would.

Artist: Jodi

Supplies: Textured cardstock (Prism); handmade paper, rice art paper, trim (unknown); iron-on transfer paper (Transfermagic); acrylic paint (Plaid); chalk ink (Clearsnap)

> Failures are just stepping stones to success in disguise. Sometimes you need to fail in order to succeed.
>
> – Lao Tze

Persevere

We're all faced with creative blunders when things don't work the way we planned. The next time your vision doesn't match your end results, I challenge you to figure out another way to try again. Who knows what you'll come up with—it may turn out better than you ever thought, and you will have overcome yet another creative pitfall. So this time, persevere!

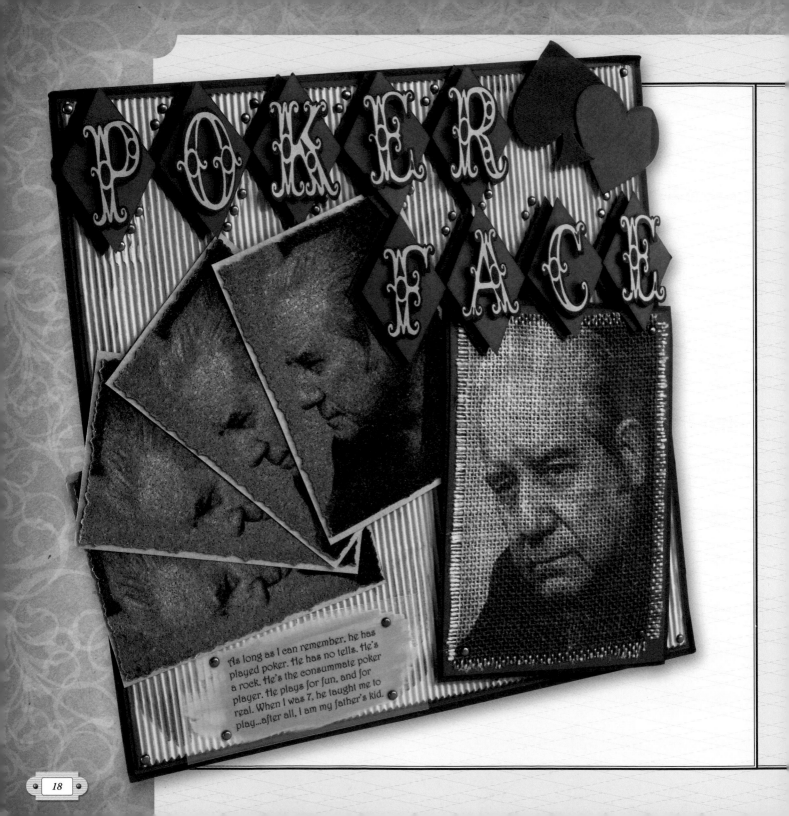

POKER FACE

As long as I can remember, he has played poker. He has no tells. He's a rock. He's the consummate poker player. He plays for fun, and for real. When I was 7, he taught me to play...after all, I am my father's kid.

Unique Photo Surfaces

You gotta know when to hold 'em...when to fold 'em...but you can only guess at what you can actually feed through your printer. I'm a texture junky. I'm also a girl who likes to push the limits when it comes to art tools by constantly "testing" them to see what they're capable of. These two qualities can be a dangerous—but interesting—combination. I decided that if something is flat enough, I should be able to run it through my printer. You would not believe what I've tried. OK, maybe you would. Many things work great...others, not so much. I'm certain, however, that manufacturers like Epson did **not** intend for their printers to accommodate materials such as burlap (which is especially challenging, but the results are cool). So, if you try putting items like ribbon, chipboard, muslin, leather, metal, cardboard, wood veneer, twill, or cork through your printer...you do so at your own risk. I do it all the time (much to the chagrin of my poor printer).

Artist: Torrey

Supplies: Corrugated paper (Xpedx); textured cardstock (Prism); brads (Creative Impressions); acrylic paint (Delta); burlap; chalk ink (Clearsnap); cork sheets; decorative scissors (Fiskars); transparency; image-editing software (Adobe)

> Life is a great big canvas, and you should throw all the paint you can on it.
> – Danny Kaye

Welcome to the Labora-Torrey!

Many of the art tools we have (though slated for one specific purpose) can be used differently. Trimmers, die-cut machines, templates, even rulers and decorative scissors can take on a whole new life if you allow yourself to experiment and find out what they can REALLY do.

Angelic Face

Milla's eyes are the first thing you notice – they are so big and bright. Then it's hard not to note the perfect round shape of her face... a face that has such a wonderful angelic quality. She's absolutely picture perfect!

Molding Paste & Glazes Background

They say control is an illusion, but I still like to have a little of it sometimes. Take this layout for example. By starting with a single sheet of white cardstock, I had control over creating the entire look and feel of my design. I could take the page in any direction my heart led. I knew I wanted soft colors and an elegant feel. From there, it developed right before my eyes.

To create my own custom paper, I applied a thin layer of molding paste through a stencil over the entire sheet of cardstock for the background texture. Once dry, I worked with gel paints to provide the color. Using a makeup sponge and a dabbing motion, I blended four different colors together until it was just the right mystical color scheme for my sepia-toned photos. After applying the colorants, I lightly sanded the raised molding paste to bring back some of the white molding paste, highlighting the texture even more. Voilà, the perfect background paper...and a deep sense of accomplishment because I had control.

Artist: Jodi

Supplies: Textured cardstock (Prism); gel paints (Plaid); molding paste (Golden); stencil (Delta); brads (Creative Impressions); metal wings, photo corners and turns (unknown); ribbon (Wrights); transparency

> Whoever I am and whatever I am doing, some kind of excellence is within my reach.
> – John W. Gardener

Take Control

Struggling to find the perfect piece of patterned paper? Stop and take control! Create your own paper using whatever you have on hand. It could be gel mediums, watercolor paints, stencils or crayons. Whatever way you choose to do it, creating your own background gives you all the control.

Columns and temples—timeless wonders of an ancient people. It's as remarkable as it is humbling... It's Greece.

Photos: Dian Carville

Cyanotype Paper

If Vincent van Gogh can have a blue period, so can I. I discovered that the paper architects use for blueprints, known as cyanotype or sunprint paper, is available in small, manageable pieces for artists. So, I ran out and got some. OK, I got a lot.

Although the instructions said to use found objects such as keys, flowers or leaves to create images, I decided there must be a way to use photographs. A few easy steps with my image-editing software were all it took to create a mask for making detailed cyanotype prints. I converted a photo to black-and-white, pumped up the contrast, inverted it to its negative, and printed it onto a transparency. Then, I laid it on top of the cyanotype paper. Following the manufacturer's instructions, I placed the paper in direct sunlight for a few minutes and followed with a quick rinse of water to stop the developing process. A little drying time, and voilà! I had detailed cyanotype prints. I was truly surprised at the details that appeared as the paper dried. It was magical.

Artist: Torrey

Supplies: Patterned paper (BasicGrey, Daisy D's, Hot Off The Press, Lasting Impressions); cyanotype paper (NaturePrint Paper); textured cardstock (Prism); border mold (Ten Seconds Studio); decorative brads (Jo-Ann); chalk ink (Clearsnap); image-editing software (Adobe); transparency; crayons

> The marble not yet carved can hold the form of every thought the greatest artist has.
>
> – Michelangelo

Inspiration Jar

Can't decide what technique or embellishment to use on your next layout? Make yourself an inspiration jar. Using little slips of paper, write down different techniques, embellishments, number of photos, layout styles, color schemes, themes, layout sketches...one item per slip. Then stick them in the jar. The next time you're stuck for ideas, just reach in and pull one (or a few) out and create a page based on whatever is written on the paper.

The
EYES
have it

They say the eyes are
windows to the soul-
and yours tell
such a sweet
and beautiful
story!

Silk-Ribbon Embroidery

At this year's county fair I was awe-struck at the amazing needlework completed by some astonishing silk-ribbon embroidery artists. Their floral patterns were so intricate and detailed. I found myself wondering how that would translate to paper, my chosen art medium.

I have been hand stitching on my pages for years now, so adding the element of silk-ribbon flowers was a fantastic way of taking that to the next level. It took some practice but before long, I was making stitches with confidence. Because the paper is so "unforgiving," it's important to pick the right stitches and draw your pattern on the paper first. It also helps a great deal to poke the stitching holes before you actually start using thread. Whether you choose to add just a few flowers or create an entire garden, you'll be pleased with the results.

Artist: Jodi

Supplies: Textured cardstock (Prism); embroidery floss (DMC); rub-on transfer (EK Success); silk ribbon (Plaid)

> Whether making art is your career or your hobby or your dream, it is not too late or too egotistical or too selfish or too silly to work on your creativity.
>
> – Julia Cameron

Go to the Fair

When was the last time you visited a state or county fair? If the answer is never or it's been awhile, then it's about time! Find the art exhibits and enjoy inspiration from all different crafts. If you're feeling really adventurous, enter a fair competition. Everyone deserves a blue ribbon at least once in his or her lifetime!

boys
WILL
BE
boys

DINNER IS SO
MUCH MORE
ENTERTAINING
WITH ERIC
SITTING NEXT
TO ME...

Polymer Clay

I have a very large stash of polymer clay in my studio. What do I do with it? Not much. That's why it's a very large stash. Although I'm fascinated by the chameleon-like qualities of this medium, it scares me. OK, it doesn't "scare" me...it intimidates me. I have books and books on cool polymer clay techniques but can't seem to bring myself to try any of them. So I decided to bite the bullet and see if I could make a layout using nothing but polymer clay. I admit, this page is very simplistic and doesn't include mind-blowing techniques that make my clay look like scrimshaw on bone with inlaid gems...but, hey, you gotta start somewhere. And, yes, even the photos are transferred onto polymer clay.

Artist: Torrey

Supplies: Polymer clay (AMACO); liquid polymer clay, shape templates (Polyform); pigment powder (Ranger); animal stamps (unknown); letter stamps (Paper Studio, Rusty Pickle); inkjet transfer paper (Lazertran); gel medium (Golden)

If at first, the idea is not absurd, there is no hope for it.
– Albert Einstein

Baby Steps

The next time you see a cool technique you'd like to try... DO IT! Dust off those technique books you have stashed away. Whether it's watercolors, polymer clay, or some form of mixed media, just go for it! Start small and as your skill and confidence build, you'll wonder why you waited so long in the first place.

FLOWER POWER

This adorable, thriving business was along the roadside on the outskirts of Lyons. You paid on the honor system by slipping your money through the window of the van. What a great throwback to the 60's.

Handmade Accents

I can't tell you how many times I have walked through the kids' craft aisle at my local discount store and wished they had this much fun stuff when I was growing up. There are so many cool things for kids to discover and play with these days. (I'm sounding way too much like my mother.)

So when Floam became the "Mom, I gotta have this!" item of the week, I was more than happy to indulge my daughter's whims. It brought her joy and gave me the opportunity to make some interesting and fitting handmade accents for this throwback-to-the-'60s page.

I was thrilled to learn that the colors mixed wonderfully and with very little hassle. The concoction was actually a lot of fun to play around with. The only trial-and-error part of the project was determining what type of adhesive would work best to keep the Floam flowers in place; I discovered it took extremely strong liquid glue. The end result…a perfect match for this flower power-themed layout.

Artist: Jodi

Supplies: Textured cardstock (Prism); ribbon (Chatterbox, Michaels, Offray); buttons (Blumenthal, Jesse James); Floam (SAS Group); corner rounder

> All children are artists. The problem is how to remain an artist once we grow up.
> – Pablo Picasso

Raid The Kids' Crafts

You'll find loads of inspiration for handmade accents in the kid's craft section at your local hobby store. Think outside the box when looking at the clays, beads, foam accents, googly eyes, pipe cleaners and the like. Nothing is off limits!

AZTEC

This tourist attraction was definitely better than most. In Mexico, this Aztec dancer (dressed in full native regalia) was striking. His performance was more than entertaining; it was spiritual. He looked like a great phoenix with his feathered headdress blowing in the wind.

Paper Piecing Technique

While sitting in a friend's office I had time to study a silkscreen print I had always admired. It reminded me of the paint-by-number paintings I did as a kid and inspired me to come up with a similar look on a scrapbook page. So, with the help of image-editing software, a craft knife, a sheet of cardstock and a whole lot of patience, I created a paper-piecing technique that mimics this look.

Using image-editing software, render the photo into colored layers by increasing the photo's contrast and applying a cut-out filter. Then, adjust the filter features to create the desired number of layers and print out several color copies of the photo onto plain paper.

Working from the background color layer forward, temporarily adhere one of the photocopies directly to cardstock and cut out each irregularly shaped color segment. Remove the photocopy, and immediately affix the cut-out piece of cardstock to the background in the correct spot. Trust me, this is the best way to assemble this. Layer by layer, the image takes shape. It's a magical process. To keep all the pieces in place, coat the entire page with a clear sealant.

Artist: Torrey

Supplies: Textured cardstock (Prism); clear sealant (Plaid); image-editing software (Adobe)

> I never came upon any of my discoveries through the process of rational thinking.
>
> – Albert Einstein

Try This!

Go to the craft store and study the paint-by-number kits. Make mental or written notes of how many layers are used to create a recognizable image. Then go home and try it yourself! Start small your first time. Before you know it, you'll be whipping out intricate paper-pieced photos that look just like their original counterparts!

kitten kaboodle

Kitten Kabootle – affectionally called "Kaboo", "Boo" or more likely, "Boo Kaboo" joined our family in early June of 2006. A coyote or fox had killed her mother, so she had been hand fed for a couple of weeks before we got her. Well, she might have had a rough start to life, but things have taken a big turn – she's now the "ruler" of the house, spoiled rotten and loved completely.

Scratch Art Photo

I recently purchased a scratch art kit for my daughter and couldn't believe how cool it looked when she was done. It inspired me to figure out how to get that same look on a scrapbook page. After some trial and error, I created this photo of my new kitten onto clay board, and I love the way it turned out.

It's very important to choose the right photo when trying this technique. Look for one with high contrast and lots of light and dark places. Once you find the right image, use image-editing software to convert the photo to black-and-white; then apply a sketch/graphic pen filter to it. Transfer the photo image onto a clay board using white transfer paper. Then it's time to play...slowly scratch your image into the clay board adding as much detail as you wish until, right before your eyes, your photo becomes a piece of art. Don't forget to apply a clear sealant to the finished project.

Artist: Jodi

Supplies: Patterned paper (SEI); textured cardstock (Bazzill, Die Cuts With A View); white transfer paper (Saral Paper); art clay board (Ampersand); chipboard letters (Making Memories); acrylic paint (Delta); clear sealant (Krylon); image-editing software (Adobe)

Everything you can imagine is real.
– Pablo Picasso

Play!

Think like a child again—find some simple craft that kids of all ages love to do. Take time today to do it just for fun. Don't expect to make some great piece of art, just rediscover the joy of creating just to create!

easy breezy
Beautiful

Rachel, I've watched you transform
from cute little girl to beautiful
young woman. There's an aura
about you... a natural inner beauty
that shines outwardly. You truly
are easy, breezy...beautiful.

Batik/Resist Technique

Being a child of the sixties, I've always loved the look of batik. But every time I tried the batik technique, I found it to be messy and, well, unpredictable. I wanted to see if I could create a batik look on a photo...but how? During my experimentation I found four different ways to do it. They all worked well, but for this layout I chose the simplest way—stamping and heat embossing with clear embossing powder. The technique isn't new; card makers have been doing it for years. But to do it with a photograph—that's new. By stamping blank cardstock and embossing it with ultra fine powder, I created a flexible, flat backdrop that easily ran through my printer. Once printed, I simply wiped the embossed areas with a damp cloth to remove the ink. Voilà...instant batik without the mess. What are the other methods I discovered? Clear lacquer, artist's masking fluid, and paper mask cut-outs. All worked well, and all gave a different look.

Artist: Torrey

Supplies: Patterned paper (Chatterbox); textured cardstock (Prism); paisley stamps (Stampendous, Wordsworth); floral trim, scroll foam stamp (Hobby Lobby); ultra fine embossing powder (Ranger); watermark ink (Tsukineko); transparency

Imagination is the highest kite one can fly.
– Lauren Bacall

Retromania

Remember all those retro crafts we used to do? Macramé, decoupage, candle making, crocheted granny squares, even hats made from soda and beer cans. Just for fun, why not revisit these time-worn crafts and find new ways to breathe life into them. After all, everything old is new again with a little creativity.

dichroic

Glass

It amazes me how they can take a sheet of colored glass and turn it into such beautiful works of art. I was fascinated by the process, so when we found some local artists with a studio, I was thrilled when they offered to let us come see how they create their jewelry. It was awesome to watch their creative process and I loved seeing all the trays full of wonderful dichroic glass pieces.

Faux Dichroic Glass

There is something so fascinatingly beautiful about watching the way glass fuses together to form these amazing mounds of colorful elegance. I've always had a weakness for the distinctive beauty of dichroic glass. But let's face it: it's a long and expensive process—one better saved for stunning jewelry. But somehow, I wanted to come up with a way of getting the look of dichroic glass to display in my scrapbook. It only took a little experimentation before I had a close reproduction of the real thing.

I started with pieces of sanded sea glass in several different colors. I applied a very thin coat of crystal lacquer to the top of the stone, then placed small pieces of iridescent plastic paper into the lacquer. I then added another coat of lacquer on top. It took some time to dry, but once hardened, I applied another coat of lacquer to the top, sides and bottom of the glass. While it might be faux dichroic glass, it certainly has the same beautiful properties of the real thing and makes a great addition to this layout.

Artist: Jodi

Supplies: Patterned paper (unknown); iridescent paper (Cardeaux Trimmings); lettering stencil (Gone Scrappin'); crystal lacquer (Sakura); foamcore; sea glass

Take a Field Trip

This layout was inspired by a trip to a local art studio where two fabulous artists were creating this dynamic jewelry. The next time you are feeling less than creative, find a local artist who is willing to share his or her craft with you. Spend the day learning new secrets, design strategies and processes. Some of the most inspiring people could be living right around the corner.

There Are No Rules

Ways to stretch, bend and break the rules

R ules? Rules? We don't need no stinking rules! We all know there is a time and place for rules and regulations—but not here…not when it comes to creating. Where the creative expression of the spirit is involved, not only are rules unnecessary, they're actually counterproductive. And, when it comes to scrapbooking, shattering imposed expectations is exactly what feeding our creativity is all about. Unfortunately, breaking rules can take us out of our comfort zones and this, for some, can be an uncomfortable place to be. Think of it like going barefoot on the beach for the first time. At first, it feels weird and wrong…it might even hurt a little. But, before we know it, shoes become a thing of the past. So, let's take off our "rule" shoes and let the sands of creativity sift through our toes. Aaaaaaah.

CHAPTER TWO

Genuine Soul

There's a light that shines within Kellie — hard to explain — but definitely there. She has a pure love of life that shows through in all she does. Rooms really do light up when she walks in and there is no pretense behind her smile. She has a genuine soul, one of grace and charm, but also one of enthusiasm and joy. Her beauty really goes beyond the smile...it reaches her soul.

Abstract Photo Collage

When I picture a photomontage, I typically think of heritage photos printed in black-and-white or sepia tones, and intertwined to tell a historical story. But that style wasn't going to work well with these lively and youthful photos. I knew this page called for energy and vibrancy.

I found a new feature in my camera that allows me to take a burst of pictures. I loved the way it snapped shot after shot as my niece went flying by in cartwheels and handsprings. I used image-editing software to meld together the tumbling photos with just a little work on the photo edges. I printed this montage onto transparency instead of regular photo paper so that I could place it over colorful polka-dot paper, mimicking a bouncing ball through the photos. The ragged stitching lends a hand at giving this photomontage a feeling of movement that draws the eye right across the page.

Artist: Jodi

Supplies: Patterned paper (My Mind's Eye); textured cardstock (Prism); chalk ink (Clearsnap); vellum spray adhesive (Helmar); image-editing software (Adobe); transparency; sewing machine

The future belongs to those who believe in the beauty of their dreams.

– Eleanor Roosevelt

Get to Know Your Camera

It's time to grab that camera manual. Chances are really good that it has some features you haven't tried yet. Find something new about your camera and then experiment. Who knows what kind of fun tools you'll find?

pha lai – yang
(decorated cloth)

Seeing this beautiful local Thai woman weaving these detailed and unique fabrics was a fascinating sight. Her talents were extremely evident looking at the colorful display of silks cloths surrounding her, each one amazing in its own beauty.

Photo: Will Smale

Salvaging & Using Bad Photos

A travel album about a recent trip to Thailand wouldn't be complete without photos of the fascinating people met along the way. But when the photo of this beautiful woman was blurry and out of focus, I had to come up with some creative way to salvage it so this memory could be included.

Image-editing software to the rescue! By playing around with different filters of all kinds, I finally came up with a great effect. Using the posterize filter brought enough elements of this photo in focus while giving it an artistic flair.

Hand embroidering an intricate design onto cloth seemed like the perfect choice to serve as a background for this photo subject. The entire effect turned out as dramatic and beautiful as the woman in the photo portrays.

Artist: Jodi

Supplies: Textured cardstock (Prism); die-cut letters (QuicKutz); embroidery pattern (Leisure Arts); embroidery floss (DMC); image-editing software (Adobe); fabric; decorative cord

Creativity is allowing yourself to make mistakes. Art is knowing which ones to keep.
– Scott Adams

Just Do It!

When was the last time you took a photo that didn't turn out as you hoped? Well, it's time to use it! If available, try altering it using image-editing software. If that's not an option, use the photo anyway! Memories are too important to be left out just because your photos aren't perfect.

White Rock Lake, Dallas, Texas

Sunset

Rocky Mountain Front Range - Denver, Colorado

Too Much White Space

There are lots of "rules" when it comes to conceptualizing the design of a layout. I like to think of design rules merely as suggestions—and in my book, suggestions are optional. Take white space for instance. Simply put, white space is unused or blank space in a design or composition. There is a lot of discussion about balancing the use of white space to create a pleasing layout. Not enough, and your page looks chaotic and cluttered. Too much, and your layout looks lacking and unfinished. Hogwash! I really like the way the white space on this layout mimics the sky with a setting sun. But some would say that having over half a page of white space is just not cool.

Don't be afraid to experiment with the use (or lack) of white space on your layouts. Allowing yourself to just go with the flow will help your creativity flow as well. Remember, you're the only one your layout has to please.

Artist: Torrey

Supplies: Patterned paper, rub ons (Chatterbox); textured cardstock (Prism); brads (Making Memories)

The real voyage of discovery consists not in seeking new landscapes, but in having new eyes.
– Marcel Proust

Field Trip

When was the last time you visited a gallery or art museum? It's time to go and soak up the creativity that dwells there. But this time, pay attention to how artists use white space in their creations. Make sure you look at many styles—classical, modern, impressionist; they all use white space differently.

Lasting Impression

When we met, there was something about you. Your looks didn't dazzle me. It was the essence of who you are that shined through. You made a lasting impression on my heart that will most certainly last a lifetime.

Optical Illusion

To look at this page without knowing what's going on, it looks very simple but very weird. Not everything is as it seems…

I've always been mesmerized by optical illusions. My favorite of this visual chicanery is the afterimage. What's an afterimage? Simply put, it's what happens when we stare at a color for an extended period of time. The cones (color sensing cells in our eyes) get fatigued and temporarily "burn out." If, after staring at a color for an extended period, you then immediately look at a blank white space, and allow your eyes to relax their focus, you'll see the exact opposite colors of what you were staring at. It does take some practice. But, once you've learned to do it, it's an amazing thing. To accomplish this with this layout, place your focus on either the photo or the white heart for 30-45 seconds. Then shift your gaze to a blank wall or a sheet of white paper and experience the magic for yourself.

Artist: Torrey

Supplies: Textured cardstock (Prism); image-editing software (Adobe)

> Simplicity is the highest quality of expression. It is that quality to which art comes in its supreme moments.
>
> – Lao Tze

The Eyes Have It

Optical illusions are a great way to help you see (and think) differently by stimulating different areas in your brain. Here's a Web site with cool optical illusions to fire up that creative side of your brain: www.mindfake.com.

This photo really says it all —

I asked if I could take some photos of you because

I wanted to do a page about how much I love you.

I should have known —

Getting you to be still and serious was just too much.

So, it was only fitting that I put this photo front and center.

After all, it's one of the things that I love about you the most —

You can always make me smile!

you make me... smile

Photo Manipulation/Altering

Goofy and my husband just seem to go together. So, when I set out to create a layout about this crazy man I chose to marry, keeping it playful was most important. I loved the idea of manipulating this silly photo of him to give it a little more personality.

By using image-editing software and adding several filters on top of each other, I found just the right combination of cartoon and poster elements to achieve the look I was after. It added style and flair befitting of such a unique photo and enhanced the mood of the entire layout. Splashing lots of color, some small details and heartfelt journaling brought this layout together in no time.

Artist: Jodi

Supplies: Patterned paper (Crafters Corner, Heidi Grace); chipboard letters (Making Memories, Pressed Petals); brads (Making Memories); image-editing software (Adobe); acrylic paint (Delta)

The one important thing I have learned over the years is the difference between taking one's work seriously and taking one's self seriously. The first is imperative and the second is disastrous.

– Margot Fonteyn

Create!

Find a photo of someone you love. If you have image-editing software, try adding some filters to see if you can capture something about their personality by altering and playing. If you're digitally challenged, use your ink pad, permanent marker or paint brush to add interesting details to enhance the characteristics you're shooting for. WARNING: Altering photos can be addictive!

Big Tex, corny dogs and corn-on-the-cob. These three things, alone, say 'State Fair' to me. Oh! How could I forget the dancing chickens? For a quarter you could either see them do a Pavlovian shimmy-shake to the timeless whine of a snake charmer's tune, or challenge one to a riveting game of tic-tac-toe. Surprisingly, the chickens usually won. Sadly, P.E.T.A. freed the performing poultry from their vending machine prisons. I miss those chickens.

State Fair

Texas

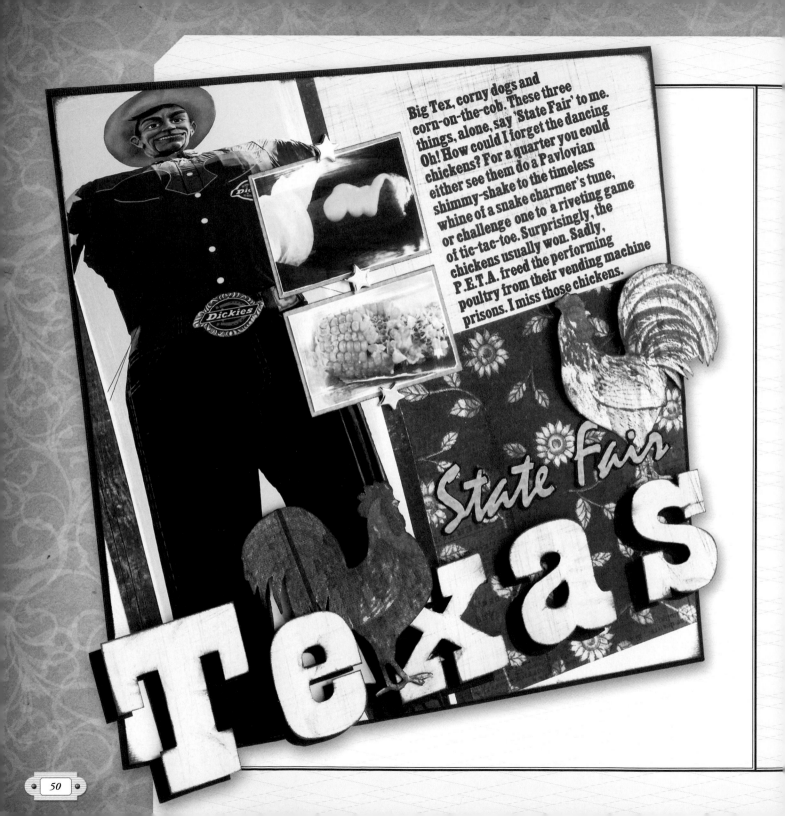

Bleeding Elements Off the Page

From a very early age we're taught, as young artists, to stay within the lines. But, as an old artist, I say NONSENSE! Lines are one of those artificial boundaries that stifle creativity. Some might even say they're a conspiracy to undermine the whole art kingdom. In my layout of the Texas State Fair, I ran all sorts of stuff outside the "lines." Heck, even the color-blocked background and focal photo are tilted off-plumb and run off the page. Exceeding boundaries not only gives us, as artists, a true sense of freedom, it adds a sense of drama, interest and movement to our creations.

Artist: Torrey

Supplies: Patterned paper (Daisy D's, Lasting Impressions, Paper Patch); textured cardstock (Prism); star brads (Creative Impressions); chalk ink (Clearsnap); image-editing software (Adobe)

COME TO THE EDGE.
We might fall.
COME TO THE EDGE.
It's too high!
COME TO THE EDGE!!
And they came,
and he pushed...
and they flew.

– Christopher Logue

Comic Book Hero!

One place you'll find great examples of bleeding elements off a page is in comic books, especially action series. Go "borrow" your kid's action hero comic and let inspiration for your next page hit you...BAM, WHACK, SOCKO!

LoriKeets

The new lorikeet exhibit at the zoo is bound to become a favorite of ours. It's so different from the other exhibits because you can become part of the experience. You can go inside the enclosure and help feed the birds. You can buy small cups of nectar that the lorikeets just love. They are a little shy at first, but it's easy to coax them onto your hand or onto your shoulder... especially when they know you have the nectar. Once you earn their trust, they'll stay and drink as long as you let them. It is such a great experience and so different from any other exhibits at the zoo.

Organic-Shaped Page

I am a firm believer that challenging myself while I scrapbook is of the utmost importance. That's when I find I do my best and most innovative work. So on this day, my self-imposed challenge was to create a page in some shape other than a square or rectangle. I found it a delight to stretch my mind and ability in such a simple way.

Finding balance, cropping photos, getting journaling to fit…all these things forced me to think in new directions. It opened up my creative thought process and gave me new perspective on the way I was creating. I found it challenging, but also extremely rewarding in the end. It broke through some old barriers that I was unaware I even faced.

Artist: Jodi

Supplies: Textured cardstock (Die Cuts With A View); circle punch

Creativity requires the courage to let go of certainties.

– Erich Fromm

Go Round!

It's your turn to break free from the straight lines and angles. Give round a try! Work with the shape instead of fighting it and allow yourself to delight in the challenge of something new.

It's called the Cow Parade. 100 life-sized fiberglass cows, lovingly decorated by local artists. They're found grazing all over town. It's a mooving experience.

Stegobovus

moo

CrOWchet

COLORado Cow

Jumper's Night Off

Jacques Moosteau

Colorado Stamp(ede)

Get Along Little Doggy

Splendid Belle

Fifty Moo Eighty

Identity Crisis

Cow Chips

moo

Cowversity

MOOticultural Cow

Moorine Life

moo

No Focal Point

When I set out to create this page I thought, "Piece of cake!" Wrong. Breaking the rules of design is not always as easy as one would guess. It's not that simple to create a page that **truly** has no focal point. I must have sketched out this layout five times before I came upon the solution. Actually, the inspiration for this layout came from a Frank Lloyd Wright window. But I decided that in order for a layout to truly have no focal point, it had to be ambiguous with regard to its direction, too. Interesting concept…a page that has no up, no down, no top, no bottom…cool. This is the result.

Artist: Torrey

Supplies: Corrugated paper (ANW Crestwood); textured cardstock (Prism); image-editing software (Adobe); adhesive application machine (Xyron); transparency

> If you follow all the rules, you miss all the fun.
> – Katherine Hepburn

On The Lookout

Inspiration can come from anywhere and everywhere. Keep your eyes (and mind) open to shape, form, style, color, and concept in your everyday surroundings. Even something as unassuming as a chair or a window may provide you with that creative spark.

Confession #22: I love the zoo!

It's true, I'm just a kid at heart — the zoo thrills me. I adore seeing all the animals and it doesn't seem to matter how many times I see them, they still excite me. Although I love them all, I definitely have my favorites — the polar bears, the lions, the seals — and each time I visit the zoo, I fall in love with them all over again.

DENVER ZOO

We've gone several times already this year and just renewed our membership. It's something we do every year. We don't seem to go as often during the winter, although I love seeing the zoo blanketed with snow. (Mental note — we must visit the zoo during a snowfall this coming winter.)

Changing the Focal Point

I have a new play toy! After years and years of wanting and craving, I finally got the camera I've been coveting. Within the first week after splurging on this "necessity," I headed to the Denver Zoo. Hundreds of photos later, I was perplexed to find myself with the challenge of choosing a favorite photo for the focal point of my zoo-themed layout. In my book, that's just another excuse to break the rules! Who says the focal point on a scrapbook page has to be a photo?

I re-created the zoo's emblem by downloading a picture of it from the Internet and making it into a paper-pieced replica. I made the choice to have the zoo emblem draw the reader's eye directly across the page. I am extremely happy with the way this gives each great photo the same weight and importance on this layout.

Artist: Jodi

Supplies: Textured cardstock (Die Cuts With A View, Prism); eyelets (Creative Impressions); foam spacers

Don't worry about failure. Worry about the chances you miss when you don't even try.
– Unknown

Start Saving!

Each one of us, as the self-appointed record keeper for our families and ourselves, deserves a camera worthy of that assignment. Start a savings fund to upgrade or add to your camera equipment. It really makes all the difference, and it's worth every penny.

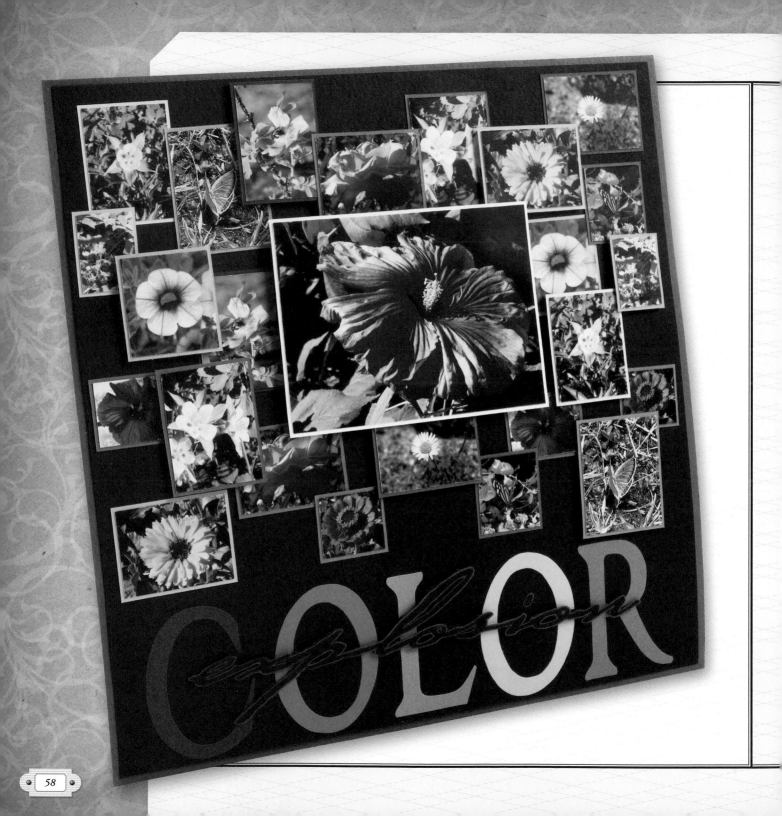

No Journaling

It's time for confessions...I love computer games! Not the intricate, time-consuming kind—just the mindless, kill-a-few-minutes type. And Mah Jong tiles is one of my favorites. One sleepless night while I was aimlessly playing this game, the inspiration hit me—the idea of making a page in the style of a Mah Jong board. That's when Color Explosion was conceived.

Once I had the photos chosen, printed and arranged, I just loved the look of the layout. I knew what I wanted to title it and how I wanted to do the title, but my problem was that it left no room for journaling. I struggled with this for quite a while when I realized this was the time to break the rules. This page didn't need journaling! It was totally complete without it. No words are needed; the photos speak for themselves. That's when I called it done.

Artist: Jodi

Supplies: Textured cardstock (Bazzill, Prism); foam spacers

> It's the good girls who keep the diaries; the bad girls never have the time.
> – Tallulah Bankhead

Take a Break

Some time or another, we are all hit with scrapper's block, and we all handle it differently. The next time you're sitting with your page in front of you and nothing seems to be coming together, walk away! Go do something totally mindless for thirty minutes. Even a brief time away can make quite a difference.

Don't let his gruff exterior fool you. Richard may look like a grizzled old pirate on the outside, but on the inside he has a heart of gold. He's one of the nicest people I know. When I told him about how I was going to put flowers and ribbons on this layout of him, he responded, "Torrey, that's disgusting, Eew gross!" That's Richard all right... Little Mister Sunshine.

Little mister

sunshine

Photo: Dian Carville

Mixed Metaphors & Color Risks

Stereotypes are everywhere. They plague us even before we're born. If you're a girl, your world is pink and filled with kittens and flowers. If you're a boy...puppies, snails and blue are what you're saddled with. But, the beauty of being artists is that we can shatter these preconceived pigeonholes. As artists, we can do whatever we please. We have creative license to do whatever the heck suits our sense of creativity at the moment. So who says a masculine page about a rugged guy can't be pink and flowery? Not me, that's for sure.

Artist: Torrey

Supplies: Patterned paper (Paper Studio); textured cardstock (Prism); chipboard flowers (Fancy Pants); chipboard letters (KI Memories); sun charms (unknown); acrylic paint (Delta); ribbon (Michaels, Offray); image-editing software (Adobe)

If there's no fun in it, something's wrong with all you're doing.
— Norman Vincent Peale

Color Your World

Artists throughout history have bent the rules of color, especially during the Impressionistic and Post-Modern eras. Take a look at these artists' works to see how they played with color: van Gogh, Monet, Warhol, Matisse and Picasso.

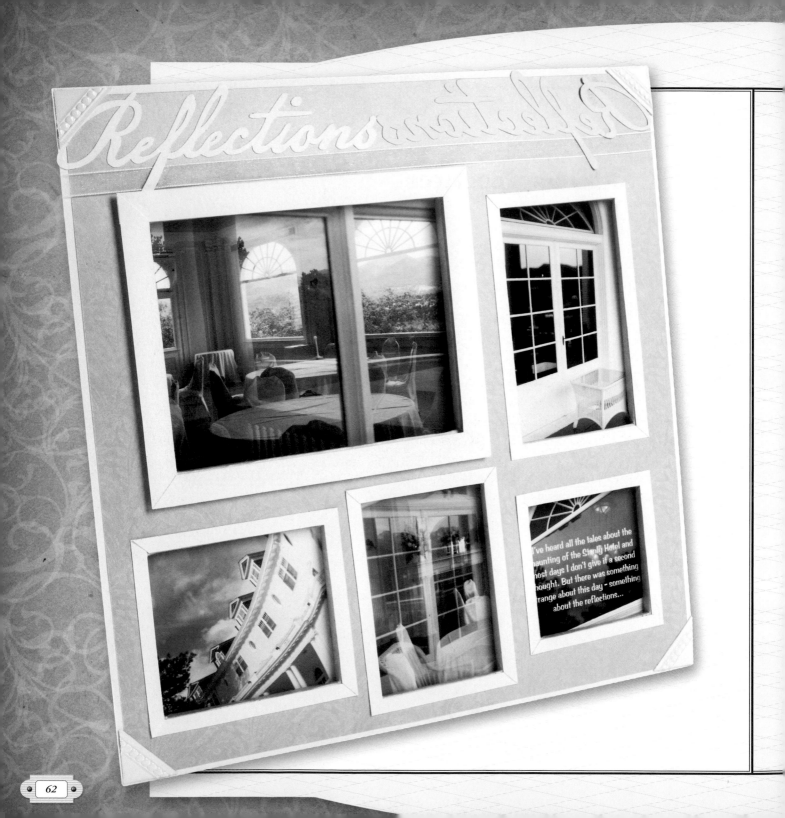

I've heard all the tales about the haunting of the Stanly Hotel and most days I don't give it a second thought. But there was something strange about this day – something about the reflections...

Photos With Strange Perspectives

Sometimes photographs never catch the most interesting angles or perspectives. We get too obsessed with taking that perfect shot, creating just the right portrait, or spending too much time worrying about the composition. All those things are important points to learn when taking photographs, but sometimes it takes an observant eye to find the most dynamic and interesting photo opportunities. Occasionally, the most unusual and appealing photos are those taken from out-of-the-ordinary angles and not-so-organized processes.

On this day visiting the stately and famous Stanley Hotel, Torrey noticed the reflection of the hotel in the back window of a van in the parking lot. When I first found her taking the photo that I used on the lower left corner, I thought, "She has finally lost it!" But something clicked in my imagination. From that moment on, I looked for every opportunity I could find to take pictures of the reflections. The photos ended up having amazing perspectives and created a mood all their own.

Artist: Jodi

Supplies: Patterned paper (Robin's Nest); textured cardstock (Prism); metal corners (Scrapworks); acrylic paint (Plaid); ribbon (Offray); foamcore

> The man who has no imagination has no wings.
> – Muhammad Ali

Change Your Perspective

Your camera's out, you've taken all the usual photos, now it's time to change your perspective. Try taking photos through a window, looking into mirrors, lying flat on your back or standing atop a ladder. You'll be amazed at some of the results and what it can do to expand your eye for creativity.

Ok, It sattred out as a ticapyl day at Six Falgs teheme prak. We wree caclebertnig Hlaey's tneth brhtadiy. One of the grlis wnetad to go on tihs relaly isanne rolelr casoter clraled the MNID EARESR (isenrt cerpey misuc hree). It was the sacerist rdie I've eevr liad eeys on. But, she relaly wnetad to go. As she and I psased by the entarcne for tihs rolelr casoter form h-e-dobule-hekocy-scitks, I toko a depe bearth and said, "I'li go wtih you." (as my sotamch sattred to cuhrn). Tihs was ISANNE! Tihs scekur geos 60 mph. In its one mlie tarck it deos two cempolte 360s, and trehe cerskrows. Nedesels to say, at the end of it my bairn was taltoly screblmad. At one pinot, I toghuht my haed was ginog to fly off. It was 60 sonceds of seher troerr. A huor letar I was in Inie aigan...dno't eevn ask me why. The sonced tmie, I atuclaly kpet my eeys oepn (srot of). But, tihs tmie I borught Jdoi wtih me. Atefr all, merisy levos capmony. My bad.

Paliyng Mnid Gmeas Wtih the Rdeear

A while back, Jodi sent me an interesting e-mail that consisted of one short paragraph. It inspired me to use this technique on a layout. Or should I say, "It isprined me." What's so "breaking the rules" about this layout you may ask? OK, the photos are kind of a funky color, but that's not so "out there." Read the journaling. Go ahead. And, no, I didn't accidentally misspell anything. What's going on? Well, the human brain is an amazing thing. As long as the first and last letter of a word are in their correct place, you can mix up all the other letters in between and your mind can still decipher it with relative ease. Dno't bilevee me? Jsut try it for yuroslef.

Artist: Torrey

Supplies: Patterned paper (Creative Imagination); textured cardstock (Prism); transparency; image-editing software (Adobe)

One must also accept that one has uncreative moments. The more honestly one can accept that, the quicker these moments will pass.

– Betty Hillesum

Stimulate Your Mind

One of the best ways to get those creative juices churning is to listen to music. Whether you take time out to sit, relax and listen with eyes closed to classical music or you just put music on in the background while you're creating, research has shown that many forms of music (classical, jazz, pop, country and ethnic) actually invigorate the brain.

The Motivation Behind

Different reasons why we scrapbook

Scrapbooking is more than just a hobby. Like the quilting bees of yesteryear, scrapbooking has created a community that bonds people together from all walks of life. Let's face it, we're all cut from different cloth. Each scrapbooker brings a different motivation to the cutting table. Many of us have pigeonholed ourselves into specific reasons why we scrapbook. We're here to tell you it's time to stretch those boundaries. Our hope is that you'll find freedom, inspiration and empowerment when you give yourself permission to scrapbook for reasons you may have not considered. **Why** we scrapbook is essential to our craft, but it isn't always about the pretty, perfect 2.5 kids and white picket fences. It can be a form of healing; a medium for expressing emotion; a tool for reaching goals; or the euphoria of creating art itself. Like the quilts of old, scrapbooking is bits and pieces of all that is us.

fresh SALAD

20 minute walk
— 2 x daily
1500 mg calcium
2 – EPA-DHA complex
— 2 x daily
2 – PhytoBalance
— 2 x daily
6 fruits & veggies daily
Decrease caffeine intake
Increase water intake

After my surgery and the resulting forced menopause, I started working with a good friend of ours who is a naturalist. It's in the hopes that I can ward off some of the negative symptoms associated with menopause. She cooked up a recipe complete with more exercise, daily vitamin and herb supplements and a change in diet. I've never had great success in making these kind of changes, but I have made it a goal to try to do as much as possible to help my body heal, gain strength and keep my hormones in balance.

Record Goals & Objectives

At forty-something years old (did I really just admit I'm that old?), I discovered a technique to help me reach a goal or objective. I find reaching for that goal becomes extremely important to me when I put it in written form. There is a mind change—a different perspective after it is documented in pen. Once I have made my mark, my commitment level becomes higher and stronger. It evolves into something I strive for, reach towards and ultimately work harder to complete.

After I learned this about myself, I decided to take it to a new level—I started **scrapbooking** my goals. If simply writing them down strengthens my resolve, how much more drive would I have if I spent the time to document them on a scrapbook page? Only time will tell, but it's been an exciting process for me so far. Plus, it is a great legacy for my daughter and future descendants. It shows the struggles and victories that make me who I am today and provides insight into what I'm trying to become tomorrow.

Artist: Jodi

Supplies: Textured cardstock (Prism); stamp (Hero Arts); chalk ink (Clearsnap)

> If what you are doing is not moving you toward your goals, it is moving you away from your goals.
>
> – Brian Tracy

Aim High

It's your turn to set a goal (something beyond doing the laundry this afternoon). Think of a real change you'd like to accomplish in your life. It could be to scrapbook more often, to shed those last few pounds, to keep a diary or to be more compassionate toward your spouse. Whatever your goal is, I challenge you to complete a layout about this objective. Let this be the motivating factor that helps you solidify its importance and gives you the push you need to see it through.

STRONGER

That which

does not kill us

makes us

STRONGER

Friedrich Nietzsche

There was a time, when I would see a woman who was being abused and I'd get angry; not at the abuser…but at her. I'd see them come into the ER, bloodied and bruised claiming they "fell". I just didn't understand how they could allow the abuse to happen. I thought they were weak, unintelligent, foolish and pathetic. I felt a loathsome pity for them—until one day, when that foolish, weak, pathetic victim …was me. I've learned that abuse is an insidious process. It starts here and there with an unkind word. At first I thought, "I know he didn't mean it." These outbursts were usually followed by apologies and flowers with promises of it never happening again. I wanted to believe…I needed to believe. But, it quickly deteriorated from there. The verbal attacks became more frequent and more vicious as my self-esteem slowly sank into oblivion. By the time it turned physical (and abuse ALWAYS turns physical in time) he controlled me. My strength was gone, my resolve --nonexistent. Some say abuse is akin to being a frog…you drop one into a pot of boiling water and it will fight to get out. But, if you put it into a pot of cold water and slowly heat it up, they'll stay in until they die. One day, when he was screaming at me, after 4 years of hell, I woke up. A light bulb went on. I realized that I didn't deserve this, that I didn't cause this. It was him. It took me learning to love myself enough to get out. I was lucky. I am alive. With the help of family, friends, my wonderful new husband and time…I continue to heal. There will always be scars, but I know I am stronger, much stronger.

Self-Discovery

In scrapbooking, it's a given that we create pages about those people who are important in our lives. So why is it we find it so hard to scrapbook about ourselves? We're very good at documenting what goes on around us, but what about what's going on within us? The journey to self-discovery is important. For one person it may be a cakewalk; for another, it's a rocky road to travel. Either way, scrapbooking can help pave the way. It's easy to wear blinders when we're looking at our own quirks, idiosyncrasies and personality traits. It's difficult to remove those blinders and look within ourselves at ourselves—difficult, but by no means impossible.

This page is a milestone for me. It marks a transition by heralding the fact that I have come far enough that I can finally document an aspect of my life that I'd just as soon forget. The quote on the layout says it all. Yep, I'm stronger all right.

Artist: Torrey

Supplies: Patterned paper, coaster elements, decorative tape (Imagination Project); textured cardstock (Prism); ribbon (Michaels); letter stamps (Limited Edition); chipboard letters (Making Memories); brads (Creative Impressions); tags; chalk ink (Clearsnap)

> Be brave enough to live creatively. The creative is the place where no one else has ever been. You have to leave the city of your comfort and go into the wilderness of your intuition. You can't get there by bus, only by hard work, risking, and by not quite knowing what you're doing. What you'll discover will be wonderful: yourself.
>
> – Alan Alda

Take a Step

It's time to turn the focus on YOU. Not all journeys to the self have to be so somber. If you're not ready to tackle the tough stuff, try writing down three of your most unique traits and do a layout on one of them. They can be silly or serious—the choice is yours!

This should have been a day of celebration, of excitement and joy...a day filled with hope, but hope was the one thing I didn't have. From the moment they told me Sarah was gone, hope died. I no longer had the dream of watching her grow up, of teaching her right from wrong and of having hope for her future.

This day was filled with every emotion in the world, but mostly we were just numb. There was a disbelief, an unwillingness to except the truth – how could this happen to us? "Why" was the word that echoed through our minds and no answers seemed to be enough to wipe away that question. This couldn't happen to us, we are good people, what did we do to deserve this, why us?

Then realization...it was happening to us! Our beautiful daughter, Sarah Kay had gone to live and dwell with the Lord. There was comfort in that knowledge, but it didn't stop the pain. There is no pain deeper, more devastating to the soul than to loose a child. I know that now. I know that I have lived and survived the worst pain I will ever know. But it's something I still have to survive everyday, for not a day goes by when I am not affected by this loss.

But, life has gone on – we have discovered joy again and have hope for our future. Haley has brought us such pleasure and comfort. She gave us a reason to get up every day, she gave us the power to stay together and she is still the most precious thing in our lives. Although there will always be something missing from our family, it is not love - our lives are full of love!

I know that the knowledge of heaven and life after death has been an amazing comfort as well. When things were at the darkest, I remembered the image of my child in the Lords arms and although the pain was still there, it brought me comfort. I know that some day I will see my dear Sarah again. I will once again hold her and in that moment, hope will be restored. I will feel the joy and celebration I missed on this day and I will rejoice in being with her. This is something I know for sure and I look forward to that day with much anticipation.

Loss

A Way to Heal

After my daughter died at birth, I was filled with immeasurable grief. I couldn't make sense of anything, and the pain took over my life. In the first few weeks that followed, I found comfort in writing. I spent hours upon hours with my journals, and discovered that writing was a way to tell her story. I think I worried subconsciously that she might be forgotten, or that the events surrounding this profound event would fade over the years.

It was then that I discovered scrapbooking. Scrapbooking gave me a way of taking all these words and the few pictures we had to record all the details and make them into a lasting memorial that could be preserved for years and years. By using this creative outlet, it allowed me the time to pour my soul into this project. It gave me time to grieve, time to remember and, ultimately, time to heal some of the wounds.

Artist: Jodi

Supplies: Patterned paper, brads, rub-ons (Chatterbox); textured cardstock (Bazzill); paper flowers (Prima); stitching template (Timeless Touches); embroidery floss (DMC); corner punch (EK Success)

> The soul would have no rainbow, had the eyes no tears.
>
> – John Vance Cheney

Heal an Old Wound

Is there something that is holding you back? Some hurt that you haven't quite let go? Although it might be one of the hardest pages you'll ever do, I challenge you to create a layout about this wound. I believe it will have a healing impact on your life.

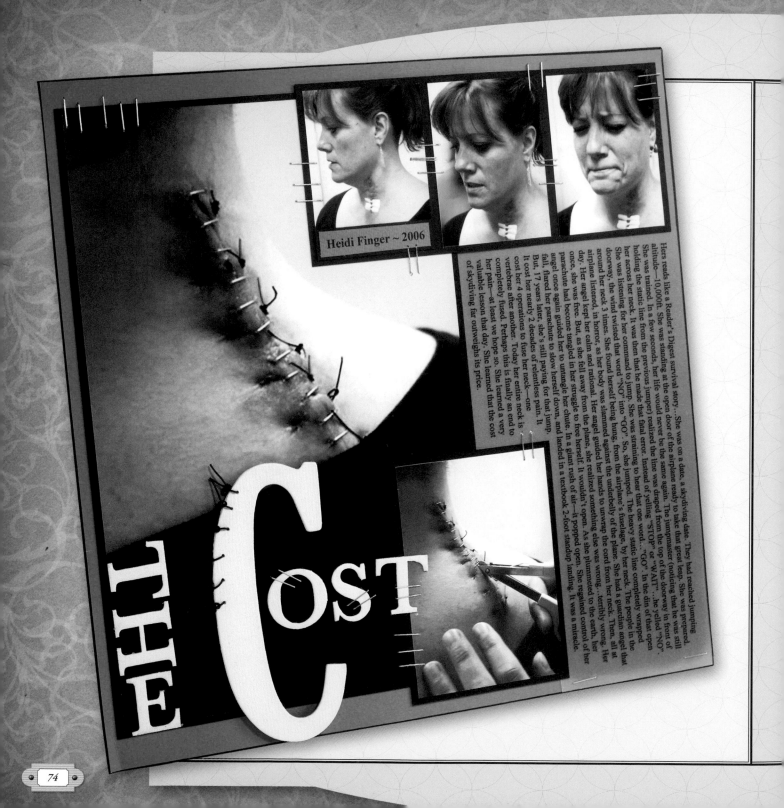

THE COST

Heidi Finger ~ 2006

Hers reads like a Reader's Digest survival story…She was on a date, a skydiving date. They had reached jumping altitude—10,000ft. She was standing at the open door of the airplane ready to take that great leap. She was prepared. She was trained. In a few seconds, her life would never be the same again. The jumpmaster (noticing that he was still holding the static line from the previous jumper) realized the line was dragged from the top of the doorway in front of her across her neck. It was then that he made that fatal error. Instead of yelling "STOP" or "WAIT"…he yelled "NO". She was listening for her command to jump. She was straining to hear that one word…. "GO". In the din of that open doorway, the wind twisted that word "NO" into "GO". So, she jumped. The heavy static line completely wrapped around her neck 3 times. She found herself being hung, from the airplane's fuselage, by her neck. The people in the airplane listened, in horror, as her body was slammed against the underbelly of the plane. She had a guardian angel that day. Her angel kept her calm and rational. Her angel guided her hands to unwrap the cord from her neck. Then, all at once, she was free. But, as she fell away from the plane, she realized something else was wrong…terribly wrong. Her parachute had become tangled in her struggle to free herself. It wouldn't open. As she plummeted to the earth, her angel once again guided her to untangle her chute. In a giant rush of air—it popped open. She regained control of her fall, flared her parachute to slow herself down, and landed in a textbook 2-foot standup landing. It was a miracle.

But, 17 years later, she's still paying for that jump. It cost her nearly 2 decades of relentless pain. It cost her 4 operations to fuse her neck—one vertebrae after another. Today her entire neck is completely fused. Perhaps this is finally an end to her pain—at least we hope so. She learned a very valuable lesson that day. She learned that the cost of skydiving far outweighs its price.

Scrapbook the Negative Aspects of Life

Some of the most significant and impacting things in life are not pretty. Many scrapbookers are reluctant, at best, to immortalize the gritty side of life for whatever reason. But as historians and archivists, it's important for us to document all aspects of life...even the not-so-appealing ones. Besides, most of us have secretly taken photos of unsavory events anyway...scraped knees from bike accidents, black eyes, a tear-stained face of someone in pain. These photos deserve to have their story told, too...maybe even more so.

I decided to do a layout about the results of my sister's skydiving accident because, after 17 years, it's still a big part of her life and who she is. It has shaped her and affected her in ways she's probably unaware of. The photos are a stark reminder that life is not always rainbows and lollipops.

Artist: Torrey

Supplies: Textured cardstock (Prism); chipboard letters (Making Memories, Pressed Petals); acrylic paint (Plaid); wire; staples

> Life is either a daring adventure or nothing.
> – Helen Keller

Bite the Bullet!

Even though it may feel "wrong," I challenge you to do a layout that reflects a part of life you may have been uncomfortable putting on a scrapbook page until now. Remember, it's only taboo if you deem it so.

LIVE

There are many people who, if faced with the cards you have been dealt, would fold, loose hope, be defeated and basically become bitter. But I am so impressed that you have taken a different road. There has been no pity party, no "why me?" mentality. You've chosen to live with gratitude, to spend precious time with those who love you and to do so many things we put off for another time.

There is a very popular song, corny but so true, called "Live Like You Were Dying". This is the choice you have made – to not fear what is ahead. After all, we know with no uncertain doubts that you have a place along side of our savior, Jesus Christ when that time comes. But for now, you're living life like we all should. Not taking anything for granted, expressing joy, seeing the pleasure in things we so often overlook. Your courage and strength are an inspiration to those who love and admire you! And you need to know that you are touching so many lives with such grace and hope

*Dedicated to the memory of Will Head
who taught us all how to live.*

Lift Someone Up

This page is my favorite in the book. Not because it's the most intriguing technique or displays the coolest new trends or interesting design, but because this page represents what scrapbooking is all about to me. To create this page, I had to push outside of my comfort zone, dig deep into my life and examine how I handle the stresses and ultimately the choices brought on by life itself.

I started out with the purest of intentions. I was going to attempt to uplift some family members I care a great deal about that are in the middle of life's greatest challenge. But this layout evolved into so much more. It was my desire to provide them with a little bit of comfort, convey some hard-to-speak emotions and let them know how much I support them in their struggles. But in the end, I was the one who was uplifted. I learned from their amazing example qualities I now lack, but desire to have. I was faced with examining my own heart and learning there are so many ways I need to grow. What better purpose could there be to scrapbook?

Artist: Jodi

Supplies: Patterned paper (7 Gypsies, Daisy D's, K&Co.); silk flowers, leaves (Prima); chipboard letters (Heidi Swapp); acrylic paint (Delta); transparency

Imagine that you are a Masterpiece unfolding, every second of every day a work of art taking form with every breath.

– Thomas Crum

Live Like You Were Dying

This challenge has nothing to do with scrapbooking—it's so much more important than that. It's time to put your life into perspective. I know it's uncomfortable, but think about the "what ifs" for a moment. What if I knew I might not be here tomorrow? What would I want to do today? Spend some time really contemplating what is important in your life and take the initiative to live like this was your last day on this earth. Life sure seems simpler and much more precious when you look at it that way.

Living with the wolf

Lupus

Look at me. Take a good, long look. Can you see it? Can you see the wolf that dwells within me? It's there all right. Just like the proverbial wolf in sheep's clothing, it lives beneath my skin. For almost 20 years this beast has been my constant companion...it never rests. It's always near. Lurking. Waiting. Always on the hunt. Always staring from the shadows. I am a modern-day werewolf. I have Lupus...Systemic Lupus Erythematosis, to be exact. Its very name strikes fear in those who hear it. But I'm here to tell that it is possible to live with this monster. There are magic potions that strive to keep the beast at bay. Pills and elixirs are the weapons I use to suppress it. Notice I said suppress...not eliminate. For there is no cure. Most people who know me on a casual level have no idea of the battles I fight on a daily basis. Most people don't know what this disease is, only that they've heard its name. So I'll enlighten these that do not know of its wrath. Lupus is a war that your body wages against itself. It's where the immune system runs amok and mistakenly marks its own tissues as being hostile invaders...and once tagged, it systematically destroys the perceived foe, one cell at a time. It spares nothing. It attacks every organ relentlessly and simultaneously. You have no idea what this feels like. To say it hurts seems grossly inadequate. I spend most of my waking hours craving rest. But, because of the pain, sleep eludes me. For me, there is no such thing as a good night's sleep. For me, feeling rested and rejuvinated is only a fairy tale. For me, pain and fatigue cling to me like my shadow. I cannot escape them. So, I have learned to live with them. I strive to keep going. Like a boxer, checking and dodging to avoid the punch that will take him to the mat...I kept moving. I was afraid if I stopped, it would be for good. So, I kept pushing myself...to the point of exhaustion. And then, about 3 months ago, I got angry and gradually stopped taking all the medications. I wanted to see just what this Lupus beast was capable of. I found out. So, I'm back on most of the medications. There are pills to control pain, pills to suppress my errant immune system, pills to fight inflammation, pills to help me sleep, pills to protect my body from all the other pills. Once again, I am armed to the teeth with little amber bottles filled with those magic beans. I try to maintain a sunny disposition...heck, I may as well, 'cuz the alternative isn't acceptable to me. But there are times I get cranky. I am, after all, only human. So, the next time you see me, look past the smile and if you catch a glimpse of the wolf, bid it hello...Cuz it's there. It's always there.

Educate Others

Part of who I am is a teacher. And as such, it's not surprising that some of my layouts are designed to educate as well as amuse. When you combine pictures with written information in an eye-pleasing package, you create a very powerful tool for sharing knowledge. Scrapbooking isn't just about preserving your family's legacy...anymore.

This layout is designed to impart a lot of information. It's sort of like a textbook laced with personal experience. I wanted to create a piece that grabs my audience visually, then engages them with journaling that is not only factual, but meaningful as well. We all have experiences in our lives that could greatly benefit others who are going through similar situations. What better way to pass on what you know than through scrapbooking?

Artist: Torrey

Supplies: Textured cardstock (Prism); transparency; image-editing software (Adobe)

> Creativity is a type of learning process where the teacher and pupil are located in the same individual.
>
> – Arthur Koestler

Reach Out

Sharing what we know and giving back to the community is good for the soul. I invite you to scrapbook an educational layout then find an organization, support group, club or institution to donate it to. By doing this you may help someone else. Think of it as "paying it forward."

I find it funny that it's so easy for me to tell my husband and daughter that I love them, we say it over and over through the day. And I try not to end a phone call with my parents without telling them the same thing. I can easily express my feelings to so many people that I love without reservation. Why is it with my brother, it's so hard to say these words?

That's why I wanted to make this layout about him. Sometimes it's just easier to write about my emotions – bringing them to life through written words – then it is to actually speak of them. But I wanted Kent to know how much I love and appreciate him.

We didn't really grow up together because there are so many years between us. He left the house when I was still very young. And a lot of my adult life, he lived on the eastern coast so we didn't have much time together. But now, with him living close by, I have gotten to know him, to learn from him, to learn what kind of man he is. I have learned to appreciate and respect him as a father, a husband, a friend and a brother.

So, as hard as it is to say it to him in person, I still want him to know...

Kent, I love you!

kent.

Work Hard
play harder

Communicate Feelings You Can't Verbalize

I've never been one who has had trouble showing emotion, voicing her opinion or speaking her mind. That's just who I am. But sometimes I find it is easier to communicate a deep feeling through writing. There is a freeing sense when you know you can say anything without having to actually physically speak the words. That's the way it was with this layout about my brother. I found it was easy to express to him all the ways he has touched my life when I didn't have to formulate the sentences while in his presence.

It might be a shame that I can't tell my brother these things face-to-face. But an even bigger shame would be if I couldn't share these emotions with him at all. Scrapbooking became the bridge to overcome this hurdle...and who knows? Maybe someday very soon, this layout will open the door that makes the words easier to find and easier to speak.

Artist: Jodi

Supplies: Patterned paper, chipboard elements, letters, paper ribbons (Imagination Project); brads (Creative Impressions); transparency

And the trouble is, if you don't risk anything, you risk even more.

– Erica Jong

Write It Down

Is there someone who has made an impact on your life, but whom you have never told? No matter how uncomfortable it may be, it's time to write them a letter. You may or may not choose to send it, but I want you to experience the freeing sense you get when you communicate those feelings through writing. It does wonders for the soul!

ANGST

One day I woke
to find the boy
I knew and loved....
had gone away.

And in his place
a brooding soul....
clandestine, dark,
had come to stay.

He seldom speaks,
his eyes – concealed
he rarely smiles....
a dark mirror.

Not quite a man,
no more a child....
he falls between
the night and day.

One day I woke
to find the boy
I knew and loved....
had gone away.

Accepting Change

Whether it's sudden or gradual, change is inevitable. Whoopee. Even when change is for the good, it's sometimes hard to embrace. It's so much easier for things to remain status quo. But status quo can also mean stagnation. And stagnation is a creativity killer. Change is an integral part of our world and can be a necessary means to a creative end.

When my nephew hit adolescence head-on with both barrels blazing, it took me by surprise. One day he was a sweet, happy boy. Overnight he became a brooding, sullen teenager. This change was difficult to comprehend, let alone adjust to. So I turned to scrapbooking to help me express what I couldn't put into words. First I took a photo of him as he really is. From there, the layout just evolved. It wasn't planned or sketched out in advance. The photo, in turn, spawned the poem and the colors were carefully chosen to further the feeling I was trying to convey. Before I knew it, this powerful layout was born to tell the story I couldn't otherwise verbalize.

Artist: Torrey

Supplies: Textured cardstock (Prism); acrylic paint (Plaid); brads (Creative Impressions); chalk ink (Clearsnap); transparency

> You need chaos in your soul to give birth to a dancing star.
> – Friedrich Nietzsche

Mix It Up

Change is one of the things that fuels creativity. So when you're feeling trapped, blah, uninspired or at odds with your surroundings...it's time to change your scenery. Take a walk, visit a friend's scrapbooking studio, or sit in a park. Changing what we're looking at can help change our perspective on many things.

Simple Things

After a week of receiving really bad news I needed to scrap a photo that just made me feel good. This reminds me of how important even the simplest of things can be – picking flowers with Haley brought smiles, laughter and sunshine into my day. I need to remember how valuable even the smallest of events can be. I found out this week that two people I care a great deal about have both come down with very advanced cancer. So, I haven't been in a great frame of mind. I surfed this gratitude album to help remind me of all of the good things in my life, to give me better perspectives – and this week I definitely needed reminding. So, I chose this photo – a bright, cheery, happy moment that didn't cost us money. I didn't take much effort, we didn't have to travel across the country and we didn't need anything else – just a quick moment to go cut flowers in the back yard with my daughter. It makes me realize how very lucky I am. My life if truly blessed.

Gratitude number 52, second week of May, 2006 – acknowledging the simple things that make life so very special

Expressing Gratitude

I have always loved the idea of gratitude journals. It's such a great way of remembering all of the things that make life so great. But as a scrapbooker, I wanted to take this concept to a different level. I wanted to scrapbook with the same purpose. I made a conscious decision to start a gratitude album. It's an album that's just for me.

So when my life got cloudy, creating a page for this album allowed me to see the good things around me. Making this layout was therapeutic in every way—right down to creating the free-form textural background using molding paste, glaze and foam stamps. Using an unstructured technique like this helped relieve stress, tap into my creative side and enjoy the process as much as I enjoy the end result.

Artist: Jodi

Supplies: Textured cardstock (Prism); metal photo corners (Scrapworks); molding paste (Golden); glaze (Delta); acrylic paint (Plaid); foam stamp (Duncan); ribbon (Michaels); transparency

> What comes from the heart touches the heart.
> – Don Sibet

Start Now!

Adopt a "can-do" attitude and start a gratitude album or journal. Make goals for creating pages at regular intervals, no matter what. Looking for the bright spots in your life and scrapbooking them will not only help you cope with trying times, it will change your outlook on just about anything.

art Mannequins

As a child, I remember admiring the jointed wooden figure that sat on my mom's drafting table. Though jars and boxes of brightly colored art supplies filled her studio, it was that little wooden person that stole my heart. When I grew up and had an art studio of my own, the first thing I bought was a mannequin. Over the years, my love of artist mannequins has grown into a collection that sits atop my windowsill. You'd think after three people, two hands, a left foot, one cat and an iguana I'd be finished. But, there's a horse, with an articulated neck, that is chomping at the bit to come home to the windowsill.

Favorites & Passions

My name is Torrey, and I'm a pack rat. What can I say? I love stuff. And, anyone who has been to my house knows this to be true. We all have passions and pleasures, secret (and not-so-secret) obsessions. We collect things, display them, dust them and love them. They tell a lot about who we are and they deserve a place of honor in our scrapbooking.

My assortment of art mannequins is just one of the many "collections" that fill my home. I wanted my layout to portray a sense of warmth and richness that reflects not only the warm tones of the wooden mannequins, but the feeling I get when I look at them. Sappy, huh? I was inspired to make a hand-pieced paper mannequin as an embellishment and the coordinating patterned papers make the perfect backdrop for my warm and fuzzy tribute.

Artist: Torrey

Supplies: Patterned paper (BasicGrey, Bo-Bunny Press); textured cardstock (Prism); chalk ink (Clearsnap); organza ribbon; chalk

> One of the advantages of being disorderly is that one is constantly making exciting discoveries.
>
> – A.A. Milne

Pack Rats Unite!

It's time to pay homage to the "stuff" in your life. Whether it's your great-grandmother's purse collection, your collection of decorative spoons, or tins of your favorite tea—it's time to do a layout on your passions and pleasures.

"Mom, these things really matter!" A funny thing to say about choosing a notebook, but I heard it several times as I tried to rush Haley through the process of picking up her school supplies. I found myself getting impatient and trying so hard to just get it done.

Then after the third or forth time she said this to me, it dawned on me...to a ten year old, these things really did matter. I remembered when I was her age, picking just the right stuff was very important. Once I made that connection, our day changed. It became more enjoyable, a great time of bonding and lots more memorable.

And as I watched her walk off to school for the start of her fifth grade year, I realized there aren't that many more years to come... they go by so fast!

K 1 2 3 4 (5) 6 7 8 9 10 11 12

and she's off

Photojournalism

A common online dictionary defines photojournalism as "journalism that presents a story primarily through the use of pictures." But ask one person what it means and you will probably get a different answer than if you ask someone else. My definition is "it's scrapbooking!" Really, what else is scrapbooking if it isn't telling a story through the use of photos? What I wanted to accomplish on this page was to document the entire event—not just the end result, but all that led up to it. It is important to me that the memory of this special event with my daughter is preserved forever.

This process requires a little bit of planning. You need to remember to snap photos throughout the event you are documenting. This means taking photos while you are buying things for the birthday party, decorating the cake, greeting guests and piling up presents—not just when the birthday cake is glowing with pretty candles.

Artist: Jodi

Supplies: Textured cardstock (Die Cuts With A View, Prism); photo turns (Junkitz); brads (Making Memories)

Creativity is inventing, experimenting, growing, taking risks, breaking rules, making mistakes, and having fun.

– Mary Lou Cook

Snap away!

Now it's your turn...the next time you're planning an important event, take the time to plan your photographs as well. Write down the details that will help document everything, then don't forget to follow through and bring out the camera at each opportunity.

On the eighth day the Lord created CHOCOLATE, and it was good. On the ninth day He separated it into dark and light, and it was better.

Chocolate

HERSHEY'S

Chocolate...whether it's dark, milk, loaded with nuts or plain – it's one of my favorite sources of inspiration. Actually, it's more like the fundamental motivator. It feeds my muse, and this in turn fuels my creativity. And, science has proven that chocolate is: a natural analgesic, a strong antioxidant; heck, it can even lower blood pressure and relieve anxiety. I have no problem justifying my addiction, because I know that my scrapbooking just wouldn't be the same without it. Scrapbooking without chocolate would be like trying to fly without wings. No wonder the Mayans and Aztecs revered it as sacred. Smart people.

Photo: Robert "Scotty" Scott

Pay Tribute To What Inspires You

It's sweet, it's creamy, it's something I can't live without...chocolate. Albert Einstein said "Imagination is more important than knowledge." I believe chocolate is more important than imagination. There are many things that inspire me, and chocolate is one of them. It satisfies more than just a hunger craving. For me, it's manna for my soul. Often times we take what inspires us for granted. It's time to pay tribute to whatever it is that feeds your creativity. Whether it's a favorite sweater, a Mother's Day card your daughter made for you when she was six, or that funky nicknack you bought at a flea market. Inspiration can come in any size, shape or form.

Artist: Torrey

Supplies: Patterned paper (All My Memories); textured cardstock (Bazzill, Prism); ribbon (Michaels); floral trim (May Arts); clear lacquer (Plaid); chalk ink (Clearsnap); painted brads (Jo-Ann); transparency; foamcore

> Motivation is like nutrition. It must be taken daily and in healthy doses to keep it going.
>
> – Norman Vincent Peale

Inspiration Central

Start an idea notebook. Add sketches, magazine clippings, pictures, snippets, doodles, quotes...whatever you find inspiring. Refer to this when you feel "stuck" for ideas.

Just For You, Just Because

This page was just for me! I had no reason other than I wanted to do it. It doesn't serve some great purpose such as passing down a legacy, keeping a memory alive or documenting some important event. But I love it! And the time I spent creating it was "my" time!

I don't indulge in too many vices (except chocolate, of course), but sometimes scrapbooking is my indulgence. It's my creative outlet, combining my love for photos, paper, the written word and experimentation all into one. It gives me reason to play, to experiment with new techniques, and to feed my creative side. It's a great time to try new things, allow myself to succeed and to fail—each bringing their own rewards.

Artist: Jodi

Supplies: Metal foil (AMACO); alcohol inks (Ranger); die cutting press (Spellbinders); textured plastics (Adorn It, Fiskars); metal foil tape (unknown)

> Art washes from the soul the dust of everyday life.
> – Pablo Picasso

Reward Yourself

You've spent time scrapbooking for everyone else...now it's your turn. It's time to do a layout with no purpose other than to enjoy the act of scrapbooking. Allow yourself to indulge in the art of creating. This time it's just for you!

Outside the Album

Inspiring ideas for taking scrapbooking to the next level

As we break free from those things that have limited our ability to let go and create, it will become easier to consider traveling outside the confines of the album itself. Our philosophy is that there aren't many things that are beyond our scrapbooking reach when it comes to platforms on which to create. We offer inspiration and encouragement to start looking at objects around us with new eyes—scrapbooking eyes. There's a whole new art form emerging from traditional scrapbooking. It's called memory art. Some would say that memory art is what happens when scrapbookers run amok. We like to think it's a natural part of the creative evolution of the craft. But when it comes to creating memory art outside the album, it's definitely no-holds-barred. Heck, if it stays still for more than five minutes, we can probably transform it into art...at least that's what we like to think.

ORPHA PINES

all of my days is always the same
before i knows it winter done came

leaves on the trees has all gone away
then all a sudden spring's comin' to play

the seasons come and then they done go
the rain a howls and wind it done blow

no matter if'n the weather 'tis fair or bad
there'll always be loads a washin to be had

TOP NOTCH
SOAP SAVING

SAN
FRONT DRAIN

Washboard Wall Art

The older I get, the more precious family heirlooms find their way to me. I am blessed with an overabundance of heritage photos, not to mention the collectible treasures that accompany them. But sometimes I find myself at a loss for what to do with them. I cringe at the thought of these cherished items spending their days in boxes on shelves. Layouts are fine for most of the photos, but some simply cry out for more. I decided this heritage photo and old washboard deserved more than to remain as junk cluttering up my basement. Unfortunately, I have no details about the woman in the photo other than her name. But that didn't stop me from paying homage to her nonetheless.

Artist: Torrey

Supplies: Antique washboard; patterned paper (Daisy D's, Dèjá Views); stitching stamp (Hero Arts); printed twill (Creative Impressions); chalk ink (Clearsnap); solvent ink (Tsukineko); wooden letters (unknown); embroidery floss (DMC); image-editing software (Adobe); lace heart (Peking Handicraft); buttons; silk flower; fabric; vintage lace; safety pins; earring; clothespins; jute; cardstock

Why not go out on a limb? That's where the fruit is.
– Will Rogers

Dust Buster

It's time to dust off those heirlooms that lurk in dark corners of your house or attic. Afraid you may "damage" the photo or item? Use copies or scans of the photos, and scour antique stores and flea markets for similar objects that you don't mind altering a little.

Photos: Bruce Aldridge

Display Album

There is something so special about family vacations and the lasting memories they create. I love capturing these endearing moments on scrapbook pages and memory art, but sometimes it seems a shame to tuck them safely away in a scrapbook album to be stored on the shelf. Here's a great way to display the good times while keeping the vacation spirit alive year round.

I came upon this wonderful metal easel at a local craft store and upon bringing it home, I was delighted to discover it was the perfect size for displaying a handmade travel album. To bring a unified feel to the project, I used the same patterned papers from the album to add some decorative elements to the easel. Now, memories of sunny beaches in Mexico can warm our hearts through the cold months of winter.

Artist: Jodi

Supplies: Patterned paper (Die Cuts With A View); textured cardstock (Prism); fibers (Coats & Clark, Colorbök, Wal-Mart); beads (Jewel Craft); acrylic paint, wooden letters (Delta); glitter glue (Ranger); chipboard; metal easel

> If you are seeking creative ideas, go out walking. Angels whisper to a man when he goes for a walk.
>
> – Raymond Inmon

Show It Off

Our photos and our memories deserve a place of prominence. Find interesting ways to display your memory art in all corners of your home. These warm touches can add depth and meaning to any décor.

I remember...playing over at Dawn
and Donna's house with all that
makeup Jo had... the frosted white
lipstick was my favorite.

you won the
ship doing the
u got to meet
was so proud of you.

I remember...how we bugged mom and
dad to find hotels with swimming
pools on vacation.

Memory Jars

I'm not a great cook when it comes to home canning, but I must admit, I'm a whiz when it comes to making family preserves. Years ago I saw an idea in a women's magazine for making a Mother's Day gift by writing down memories of mom on little strips of paper and presenting them to her in a construction paper-covered can. I loved this idea—so much so that I have now made these "memory jars" for every member of my family. I don't know what part of creating these heartfelt tributes is the most fun...decorating the jars, reliving the memories as I'm writing, or seeing the expression on the recipient's face when they're presented with these "fruits" of love.

Artist: Torrey

Supplies: Patterned paper, decorative brads, letter brads (Paper Studio); textured cardstock (Prism); jars (Anchor Hocking); die-cut flowers (Spellbinders); inkjet transfer paper (Lazertran); word charms (Dress It Up); book plate, rhinestone brads (Making Memories); chipboard letters (Heidi Swapp); acrylic paint (Delta); clear sealant (Plaid); ribbon (Michaels, Offray)

> Inspiration can be found in a pile of junk. When you put it together with a good imagination, you invent something.
>
> – Thomas Edison

A Trip Down Memory Lane

Choose a special person in your life and record all the positive memories of that individual that come to mind. You'll be surprised at how many details you will recall as you write. Then you can either make a memory jar for that person or save your notes for future journaling opportunities.

Triptych Mirror

I never knew my mother-in-law, but paying tribute to the woman who shaped and molded the man I love was important to me. I knew I wanted to impart a feeling of elegance and grace in this project—something worthy of her beautiful spirit. The idea of placing her photo in this mirror struck me one day as I perused my local home décor store. The mirror was a little expensive, but I fell instantly in love with the triptych design.

To create my own personal touch, I used a straight-edged razor blade to scratch the grey paint from the back of the mirror and then used steel wool to burnish off the reflective coating. This gave me a window to display the photo. Stamping on the mirror with a solvent-based ink created the whimsical backdrop for the silk flowers and coiled wire. Touches of lace and a title completed this stunning piece that now graces our fireplace mantel.

Artist: Jodi

Supplies: Patterned paper (Junkitz); textured cardstock (Prism); stamps (Autumn Leaves, Denami Design, Hero Arts, Plaid); solvent ink (Tsukineko); beads (JewelCraft); lace; purple wire; triptych mirror

> Imagination grows by exercise, and contrary to common belief, is more powerful in the mature than in the young.
>
> – Somerset Maugham

Splurge!

Once in a while it's OK to give yourself permission to splurge. Some projects simply dictate spending more moolah. Remember, these are your memories, your family and your home…and "you're worth it!"

HEIDI

HARLEY-DAVIDSON

IT'S NOT THE
DESTINATION
IT'S THE
JOURNEY

HARLEY-DAVIDSON
MOTOR

Fly the Fury

NEAL

MO

Silhouette-Cut Board Book

While browsing the book section of my local thrift store, I came across some children's oversized board books. Some of them had been cut into shapes along their edges to silhouette the image on their covers. I love shapes with soft curves and interesting angles. But when it comes to books and albums, we're usually limited to squares and rectangles. Then a light bulb went off in my head—why couldn't I take one of these jumbo books and turn it into whatever shape I wanted? I already knew that board books make excellent platforms for mini albums. So I chose a large board book amongst the selection, brought it home and drew a silhouetted face along the edge. I then cut it out with the most heavy-duty pair of scissors I own (what I wouldn't have given for a power jigsaw).

Artist: Torrey

Supplies: Children's board book; textured cardstock (Bazzill); patterned paper (Colorbök, EK Success, Heidi Grace, Karen Foster, Provo Craft, Sandylion, Stampin' Up); dimensional stickers (EK Success); ribbon (May Arts, Michaels, Offray); letter stamps (Hampton Art); mini brads (Creative Impressions); chipboard flowers (Fancy Pants); printed transparency (EK Success); glitter glue (Ranger); chalk ink (Clearsnap); solvent ink (Tsukineko)

> What you love is a sign from your higher self of what you are to do.
> — Sanyana Roman

Tool Time

Tools aren't just for construction and home repair anymore. Many power tools can be used in scrapbooking...jigsaws, drills, miters, routers, tin snips...the list is endless. Have fun, and don't forget to wear proper safety equipment.

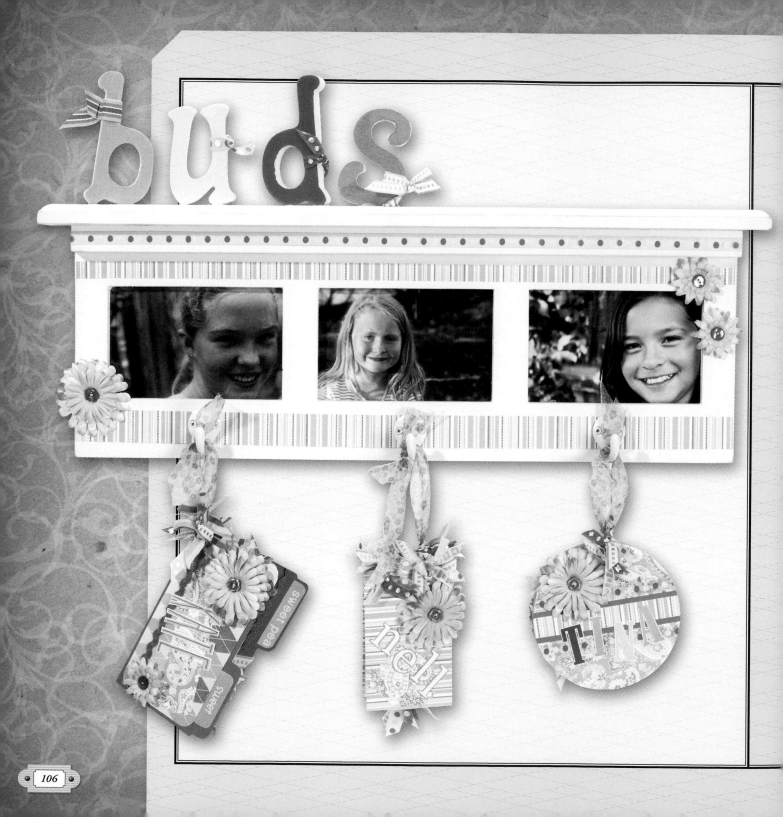

Hanging Shelf

I love a good bargain. Come on, what's not to love? A good deal is such a treat to find. I am constantly wandering the aisles of craft stores to find the bargain bins and stocking up on lots of ordinary items that need an artsy touch.

That's how this shelf came about. I don't even remember when I bought it, but I knew someday it would become a treasure. When it came time to redecorate my daughter's room, I thought it would make a great addition to the décor. It didn't take much to whip up this charming creation—just some coordinating papers, a few wooden letters and three adorable girlfriends. To display some great pictures taken over the years and to chronicle my daughter's special friendship with each girl, I hung a fun mini album under each of their photos. The finished piece turned out so cute I wish I had bought more than one shelf when I had the chance.

Artist: Jodi

Supplies: Textured cardstock (Bazzill, Prism); patterned paper (Making Memories); ribbon (Chatterbox, KI Memories, Michaels, Offray); letter stickers (Chatterbox, SEI); cardstock stickers (Doodlebug); silk flowers (Creative Co-op); wooden shelf; wooden letters; acrylic spray primer, paint (Krylon)

Friends are the family
we choose for ourselves.
– Edna Buchanan

Search for the Not-So-Obvious

Sometimes the greatest finds are in unexpected places. Take an extra 30 minutes the next time you're walking the aisles of your local craft store and visit each row. Look at all the crafts outside of scrapbooking, find the closeout bins and look for items you might enjoy altering. It's always nice to have a stash of great treasures just waiting for your creative flair.

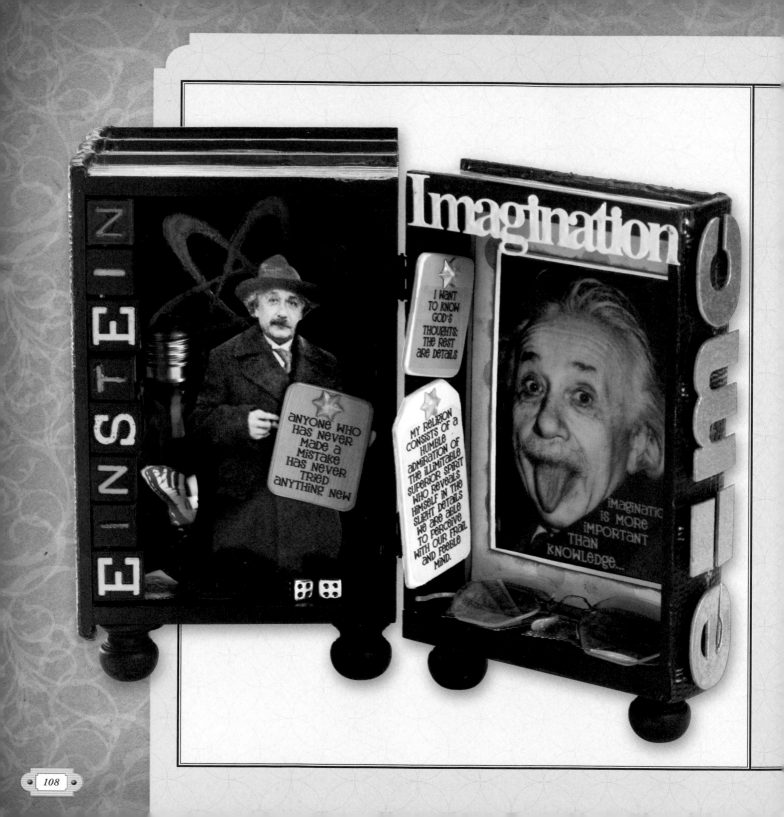

Memory Art

Although seemingly separated by a vast artistic ocean, scrapbooking and altered art lay moored in the same harbor. To me, altered art is merely a natural extension of scrapbooking. Both are collections of images and words combined to express sentiment and emotion. Basically, one accomplishes this in two dimensions, the other, in three…until now. What happens when you combine the two? Enter the newest member of the creative family—memory art. Memory art is the marrying, if you will, of scrapbooking and altered art. It offers the adventurous scrapbooker yet another venue through which to create. I love "memory art." I'm not quite funky enough to be a full-blown altered artist, but as a memory artist, I think I've found a niche. Oh, and if you turn off the lights, my Einstein shrine glows in the dark! OK, maybe I *am* funky enough to be an altered artist.

Artist: Torrey

Supplies: Decorative box (Hobby Lobby); patterned paper (My Mind's Eye); textured cardstock (Prism); Einstein stamps (Zettiology); eye stamp (Stampabilities); foam stamps (Duncan, Plaid); wood finials (Lara's Crafts); butterfly sticker, Einstein card (Paper House); light bulb jar (Michaels); chipboard letters (Making Memories); acrylic paint, clear lacquer (Delta); glow-in-the-dark paint (Duncan); chalk ink (Clearsnap); gold leafing pen (Krylon); metal charm (Artgirlz); metal word (Jo-Ann); solvent ink (Tsukineko); star brads (Creative Impressions); wooden tags (Chatterbox); antique spectacles; chalk; dice; light fixture; vintage game pieces; watch face; wire

> The whole difference between construction and creation is exactly this: that a thing constructed can only be loved after it is constructed; but a thing created is loved before it exists.
>
> – Charles Dickens

Alter Your Perception

Go alter something. You can start simply with a plain wooden box, or jump in headfirst and create art out of an old tire! Flea markets, garage sales, antique stores and even dumpsters and salvage yards are great places to find that "diamond-in-the-rough."

Dentist
Wed.
        2:30

Milk
Butter
Eggs
Sugar
Bread
Apples
Chips
Cereal
Film

Bulletin Board

The message center next to our phone is a disaster area. I have a dry erase board that's much too small and is always getting erased at the most inopportune times. I knew I needed to come up with a new system to help keep our phone messages organized—especially with a pre-teen in the house. I found this unique bulletin board in (what else?) the bargain bin. I wanted to turn it into something that would serve as a great place for our family to record messages.

The paisley flowers were inspired by a greeting card given to me by a friend. She had the great idea of using a paisley stamp to create flower petals. Once I found this wonderful paisley patterned paper in the colors I wanted, I had to use her innovative idea. The flowers on this bulletin board turned out so cute that all I needed to finish were some strands of ribbon and a few cute brads to serve double duty as the flower centers and as tacks. I could hardly wait to hang it in our kitchen to help control and organize our chaos.

Artist: Jodi

Supplies: Cloth pushpin panel (Making Memories); patterned paper (SEI); ribbon (May Arts, Michaels, Offray); brads (Bazzill, Hot Off The Press, Making Memories); glitter glue (Ranger); cloth; glue gun; tacks

The more you lose yourself in something bigger than yourself, the more energy you will have.

– Norman Vincent Peale

Permission Granted

Imitation is the greatest form of flattery and with an abundance of ideas all around, you shouldn't feel like you have to reinvent the wheel every time you sit down to scrapbook. It's OK to adapt someone else's brilliant idea into one that helps you create your own unique piece of art.

The keys of our pas
open doors of our fu
where gifts are waiting

Jewelry

Scrapbooking supplies are so beautiful and varied that it seems a shame to use them only on layouts. Wait a sec. Who says you have to? With all the gorgeous paper, embellishments, doodads and whatnots out there, I decided I could definitely use these items to make wearable art. For my necklace and earrings, I combined photos and antique keys from four generations of my family along with scrapbooking charm frames and beads made from patterned paper. The watchband is (you guessed it) constructed from patterned paper and eyelets. Making jewelry is a great way to use up all those leftover bits and pieces. And there's always some gift-giving opportunity waiting for a project like this.

Artist: Torrey

Supplies:

Keys Of My Past Necklace & Earrings: Patterned paper (Daisy D's); chalk ink (Clearsnap); frame charms, jewelry findings (Darice); chain (unknown); amulet case (Helstrom Studios); tacky tape (Provo Craft); antique keys; transparency; image-editing software (Adobe)

Sunflower Watchband: Patterned paper (Daisy D's); tacky tape (Provo Craft); chalk ink (Clearsnap); eyelets (Creative Impressions); cloth book binding tape; watchface

Whether you think you can or whether you think you can't—you are right.
— Henry Ford

Spruce It Up

Take an old necklace, chain, pair of earrings or watch and add some spice with your scrapbook supplies. Don't have any jewelry on hand? Garage sales, flea markets and thrift stores are great sources for inexpensive costume jewelry to play with.

Paper Sculpture

Let's face it, I'm a lumpy scrapbooker at heart. I love dimension and texture. So when I set out to create an out-of-the-album project, I knew I could pull out all the dimensional stops.

Enter my paper flowers sculpture. I know they look impossible—but they're relatively easy to re-create. My secret? There is no secret! Start by purchasing silk flowers from the craft store. When choosing them, pay attention to their shapes, not their color. Then, disassemble them. Go ahead, rip 'em apart. Flatten their petals and scan them to create your templates. You'll be surprised at how basic and similar the petal shapes are. Many flowers have petals of the same shape, so you can create lots of different flowers from just a few petal designs. Using your templates, cut the petals out of cardstock, shaping them slightly with a rounded object before reassembling them. Make sure you use a strong glue to hold them together. Now you're ready to create your very own floral masterpiece.

Artist: Torrey

Supplies: Shadowbox frame (Walnut Hollow); textured cardstock (Prism); acrylic paint, clear lacquer (Plaid); wire

> It's kind of fun to do the impossible.
> – Walt Disney

Creative Exercise

It's true...it's easier to buy pre-made embellishments than to create your own. But what does that do to foster and spark your creativity? Next time you want to add that special element to your project, try making it yourself. Think of it as calisthenics for that creative muse that's lounging on your couch.

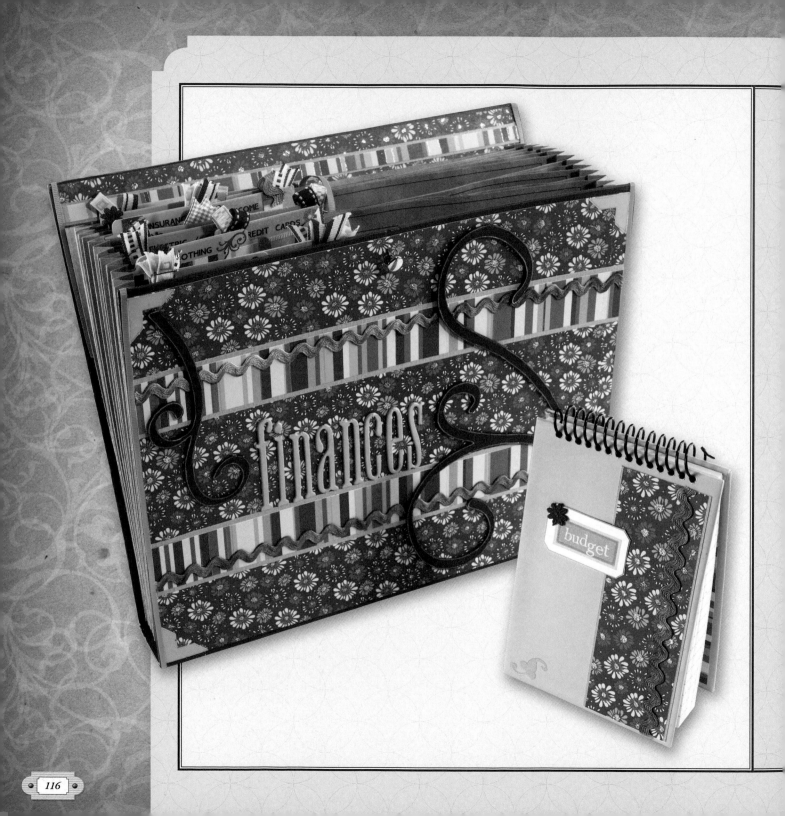

Accordion Organizer

There are very few things I like less than paying bills—and I'm sure I'm not alone on that one. So I decided to add a little sunshine into this tedious task by creating a bright and functional bill keeper.

I found an old accordion file that had plenty of slots for all the categories I needed. I added lots of fun elements including colorful ribbons, decorated labels, painted chipboard and even some glitter glue. I love the fact that I ended up with something that makes a less-than-desirable task a little bit more bearable...and keeps me much more organized in the process.

Artist: Jodi

Supplies: Patterned paper (EK Success, KI Memories); textured cardstock (Die Cuts With A View); chipboard designs (Fancy Pants); chipboard letters, colored staples, rub-on letters (Making Memories); rub-ons, tag (Chatterbox); ribbon (Chatterbox, KI Memories, Michaels, Offray); glitter glue (Ranger); glitter pen (Sakura); labels (Dymo); die-cut photo corners (QuicKutz); accordion file, notebook

> Take risks. You cannot discover new oceans unless you have the courage to lose sight of the shore.
> – Unknown

Beyond the Page

The next time you have completed a scrapbook page, don't start cleaning up just yet. Immediately use the leftover scraps to create a new piece of paper art. Add a decorative touch to an otherwise boring notebook, use your remnants to make a handmade card to give to a deserving friend, or add an artistic touch to a junkyard find.

Canvas Tote Bag

Playing dress up is something most of us did as kids. Some of us still do—but now we call it fashion. I am not exactly what you'd call a "slave" to fashion. I like funky stuff. Colorful, one-of-a-kind stuff suits me, well, to a "T" (get it?). So, when Jodi and I started brainstorming ideas for what to include in the book...I just knew there had to be something fun and playful in here somewhere. I believe that I've reached a new level in my creation when even my handbags are works of art. I can't wait to strut this tote bag en route to a crop or social gathering with scrap-happy friends. Now, if I could only convince Jodi to carry one, too. She's not as adventurous as I am when it comes to clothes and accessories...but I've got hope.

Artist: Torrey

Supplies: Iron-on transfer paper (Transfermagic); shrink plastic (K&B Innovations); die-cut flower (Spellbinders); watercolor pencils (Staedtler); felt markers (EK Success); jewelry findings, beads (Crafts Etc.); micro-beads, tacky tape (Provo Craft); rickrack (Wrights); image-editing software (Adobe); chain; canvas tote

It's always too soon to quit!
– Norman Vincent Peale

Get Your Daily Dose

Many "experts" and artists alike agree that in order to grow as artists we must create on a daily basis. Set aside a specific amount of time every day to create. Whether it be ten minutes or an hour...creating is to the artist what exercise is to the athlete. We gotta do it to stay in shape.

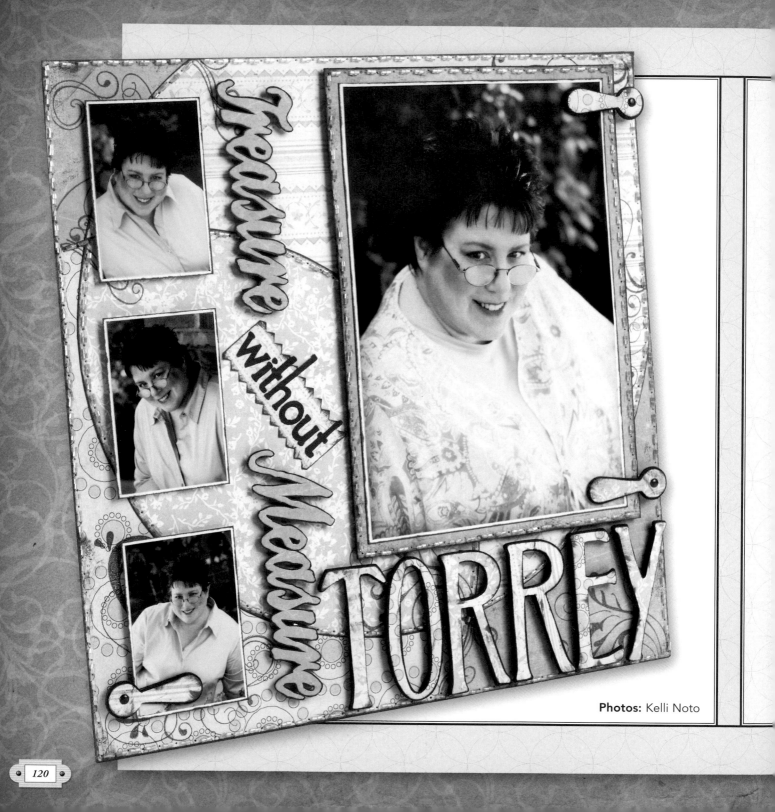

Treasure without Measure

TORREY

Photos: Kelli Noto

Those who know me well know that there are very few times when I am at a loss for words. Words normally flow easily for me. But that just isn't the case while trying to explain my admiration and love for Torrey and the importance she has in my life.

She has influenced me in so many ways…most profoundly, in who I am and how I see the world around me. She constantly challenges me to become a better person, a stronger wife and mother and a more compassionate friend. Her example is emulation for who I want to be and how I want to live my life.

OK, now that we have the mushy-gushy stuff out of the way, let's talk about her art.

I have heard her described as the MacGyver of scrapbooking, but recently another nickname surfaced (thanks, Nick)—Left Field! She really is "out there…in left field" when it comes to how she approaches her craft.

There's nothing too intimidating to try, and no art medium that can't be conquered in the quest of finding something cool for her memory art. She truly inspires me to stretch my own boundaries and thought processes. Call it competition or just good old-fashioned rivalry, but she makes me a better scrapper. Torrey evokes a strong sense of confidence in me and is always pushing me to achieve things I didn't believe possible.

We have spent many late nights dressed in PJs, with chocolate close at hand, sitting next to each other in my studio. And these are the times I treasure the most…when it's just us, doing what we love to do, sharing this great passion together as best friends, sisters at heart and more than anything, soulmates!

I love you, Torrey!

Jodi

AUTHOR TRIBUTE

No such thing as Just JODI

Photos: Kelli Noto

Just what can I say about Jodi? Well, a lot actually. What strikes me first about her is how we met. My sister, Heidi, met Jodi first. And upon meeting her, Heidi rushed home and declared, "Torrey, I've just met your best friend!" She knew from the very minute she met her, that Jodi and I were soulmates. Heidi was right. Jodi and I go together like chocolate and peanut butter. She's sweet and I'm nutty. It's a perfect match.

Whether you call it destiny, fate, or joyous synchronicity, it always seemed that we were brought together by some unseen force of the universe itself. There is a definite purpose to our friendship; a greater calling if you will. I can feel it…and the calling is not just about scrapbooking (although, come to think of it, she is the one who dragged me into this whole scrapbooking cult thing).

Over the years we've dabbled in many crafts and art mediums together. Whether she's decorating traditional Native American pottery or whipping up some delectable morsel in the kitchen, Jodi is the Midas of creative endeavors. Whatever she touches with her creative energy turns out golden.

And Jodi has a light inside her. I'm drawn to it. She's my beacon. There are a very few people on this earth whom I would want to (or could) spend every minute of every day with…she's one of them. When I'm down, she brings me peace. When I'm grouchy, she makes me laugh at myself. When I'm weary, I find rest within her spirit. She inspires me in everything I do. She's my muse. So, to me, there's no such thing as "just" Jodi. Because to me, Jodi is…everything.

Torrey

AUTHOR TRIBUTE

Source Guide

The following companies manufacture products featured in this book. Please check your local retailers to find these materials, or go to a company's Web site for the latest product. In addition, we have made every attempt to properly credit the items mentioned in this book. We apologize to any company that we have listed incorrectly, and we would appreciate hearing from you.

7 Gypsies
(877) 749-7797
www.sevengypsies.com

Adobe Systems Incorporated
(800) 833-6687
www.adobe.com

Adorn It/Carolee's Creations
(435) 563-1100
www.adornit.com

All My Memories
(888) 553-1998
www.allmymemories.com

American Art Clay Co. (AMACO)
(800) 374-1600
www.amaco.com

Ampersand Art Supply
(800) 822-1939
www.ampersandart.com

Anchor Hocking
(800) 562-0773
www.anchorhocking.com

ANW Crestwood
(973) 406-5000
www.anwcrestwood.com

Artgirlz
(401) 323-2997
www.artgirlz.com

Autumn Leaves
(800) 588-6707
www.autumnleaves.com

A&W Products Co., Inc.
(800) 223-5156
www.awproducts.com

BasicGrey
(801) 544-1116
www.basicgrey.com

Bazzill Basics Paper
(480) 558-8557
www.bazzillbasics.com

Berwick Offray, LLC
(800) 344-5533
www.offray.com

Big Art Brand
(405) 359-7777
www.bigartbrand.com

Blumenthal Lansing Company
(563) 538-4211
www.buttonsplus.com

Bo-Bunny Press
(801) 771-4010
www.bobunny.com

Canson, Inc.
(800) 628-9283
www.canson-us.com

Cardeaux Trimmings -
contact information not available

Chatterbox, Inc.
(888) 416-6260
www.chatterboxinc.com

Coats & Clark
(800) 648-1479
www.coatsandclark.com

Colorbök, Inc.
(800) 366-4660
www.colorbok.com

Crafter's Corner, Inc
(800) 390-5358
www.crafterscornerinc.com

Crafts, Etc. Ltd.
(800) 888-0321 x 1275
www.craftsetc.com

Creative Co-op
(866) 323-2264
www.creativecoop.com

Creative Imaginations
(800) 942-6487
www.cigift.com

Creative Impressions
(719) 596-4860
www.creativeimpressions.com

Daisy D's Paper Company
(888) 601-8955
www.daisydspaper.com

Darice, Inc.
(800) 321-1494
www.darice.com

Dèjá Views
(800) 243-8419
www.dejaviews.com

Delta Technical Coatings, Inc.
(800) 423-4135
www.deltacrafts.com

Denami Design Rubber Stamps
(253) 437-1626
www.denamidesign.com

Die Cuts With A View
(801) 224-6766
www.diecutswithaview.com

DMC Corp.
(973) 589-0606
www.dmc-usa.com

Doodlebug Design Inc.
(877) 800-9190
www.doodlebug.ws

Dress It Up
www.dressitup.com

Duncan Enterprises
(800) 438-6226
www.duncanceramics.com

Dymo
(800) 426-7827
www.dymo.com

EK Success, Ltd.
(800) 524-1349
www.eksuccess.com

Fancy Pants Designs, LLC
(801) 779-3212
www.fancypantsdesigns.com

Fiskars Brands, Inc.
(866) 348-5661
www.fiskarscrafts.com

Golden Artist Colors, Inc.
(800) 959-6543
www.goldenpaints.com

Gone Scrappin'
(435) 647-0404
www.gonescrappin.com

Hampton Art Stamps, Inc.
(800) 229-1019
www.hamptonart.com

Heidi Grace Designs, Inc.
(866) 348-5661
www.heidigrace.com

Heidi Swapp/Advantus Corporation
(904) 482-0092
www.heidiswapp.com

Helmar
www.helmar.com.au

Helstrom Studios -
contact information not available

Hero Arts Rubber Stamps, Inc.
(800) 822-4376
www.heroarts.com

Hobby Lobby Stores, Inc.
www.hobbylobby.com

Home Depot U.S.A., Inc.
www.homedepot.com

Hot Off The Press, Inc.
(800) 227-9595
www.b2b.hotp.com

Imagination Project, Inc.
(888) 477-6532
www.imaginationproject.com

Jesse James & Co., Inc.
(610) 435-0201
www.jessejamesbutton.com

JewelCraft, LLC
(201) 223-0804
www.jewelcraft.biz

Jo-Ann Stores
www.joann.com

Junkitz
(732) 792-1108
www.junkitz.com

K&B Innovations, Inc./Shrinky Dinks
(262) 966-0305
www.shrinkydinks.com

K&Company
(888) 244-2083
www.kandcompany.com

Karen Foster Design
(801) 451-9779
www.karenfosterdesign.com

KI Memories
(972) 243-5595
www.kimemories.com

Krylon
(800) 457-9566
www.krylon.com

Lara's Crafts
(800) 232-5272
www.larascrafts.com

Lasting Impressions for Paper, Inc.
(800) 936-2677
www.lastingimpressions.com

Lazertran
(800) 245-7547
www.lazertran.com

Le Bouton -
contact information not available

Leisure Arts/
Memories in the Making
(800) 526-5111
www.leisurearts.com

Limited Edition Rubberstamps
(800) 229-1019
www.limitededitionrs.com

Magenta Rubber Stamps
(450) 922-5253
www.magentastyle.com

Making Memories
(801) 294-0430
www.makingmemories.com

May Arts
(800) 442-3950
www.mayarts.com

Michaels Arts & Crafts
(800) 642-4235
www.michaels.com

My Mind's Eye
(866) 989-0320
www.mymindseye.com

NaturePrint Paper
www.natureprintpaper.com

Offray- see Berwick Offray, LLC

Paper House Productions
(800) 255-7316
www.paperhouseproductions.com

Paper Patch, The
(800) 397-2737
www.paperpatch.com

Paper Studio
(480) 557-5700
www.paperstudio.com

Peking Handicraft, Inc.
(800) 872-6888
www.pkhc.com

Plaid Enterprises, Inc.
(800) 842-4197
www.plaidonline.com

Polyform Products Co.
(847) 427-0020
www.sculpey.com

Pressed Petals
(800) 748-4656
www.pressedpetals.com

Prima Marketing, Inc.
(909) 627-5532
www.primamarketinginc.com

Prism Papers
(866) 902-1002
www.prismpapers.com

Provo Craft
(800) 937-7686
www.provocraft.com

PSX Design
www.sierra-enterprises.com/psxmain

QuicKutz, Inc.
(888) 702-1146
www.quickutz.com

Ranger Industries, Inc.
(800) 244-2211
www.rangerink.com

Robin's Nest Press, The
(435) 789-5387
robins@sbnet.com

Rusty Pickle
(801) 746-1045
www.rustypickle.com

Sakura Hobby Craft
(310) 212-7878
www.sakuracraft.com

Sandylion Sticker Designs
(800) 387-4215
www.sandylion.com

Saral Paper Corp.
www.saralpaper.com

SAS Group, Inc.
(920) 966-6600
www.shopsas.com

Scrappy Cat, LLC
(440) 234-4850
www.scrappycatcreations.com

Scrapworks, LLC/As You Wish
Products, LLC
(801) 363-1010
www.scrapworks.com

SEI, Inc.
(800) 333-3279
www.shopsei.com

Spellbinders Paper Arts, LLC
(888) 547-0400
www.spellbinders.us

Staedtler, Inc.
(800) 776-5544
www.staedtler.us

Stampabilities
(800) 888-0321
www.stampabilities.com

Stampendous!
(800) 869-0474
www.stampendous.com

Stampin' Up!
(800) 782-6787
www.stampinup.com

Stamps by Judith
www.stampsbyjudith.com

Technique Tuesday, LLC
(503) 644-4073
www.techniquetuesday.com

Ten Seconds Studio
www.tensecondsstudio.com

Timeless Touches/Dove Valley
Productions, LLC
(623) 362-8285
www.timelesstouches.net

Transfermagic
(800) 268-9841
www.transfermagic.com

Tsukineko
(425) 883-7733
www.tsukineko.com

Wal-Mart Stores, Inc.
(800) 925-6278
www.walmart.com

Walnut Hollow Farm, Inc.
(800) 950-5101
www.walnuthollow.com

We R Memory Keepers
(801) 539-5000
www.wermemorykeepers.com

Wordsworth
(877) 280-0934
www.wordsworthstamps.com

Wrights Ribbon Accents
(877) 597-4448
www.wrights.com

Xpedx
(513) 965-2900
www.xpedx.com

Xyron
(800) 793-3523
www.xyron.com

Zettiology
www.zettiology.com

Additional Supplies List

ToJo Mojo: Page 6

Supplies: Textured cardstock (Paper Studio, Prism); ribbon (unknown); buttons (Blumenthal, Junkitz, Karen Foster, Lasting Impressions, Le Bouton)

Treasure Without Measure: Page 120

Supplies: Patterned paper (BasicGrey); textured cardstock (Bazzill); chipboard letters (K&Co.); chipboard photo corners (BasicGrey); acrylic stamps (Autumn Leaves); chalk ink (Clearsnap); beads (A&W Products); brads (Creative Impressions); invisible thread; decorative scissors (Fiskars)

Just Jodi: Page 122

Supplies: Patterned paper (We R Memory Keepers); textured cardstock (Bazzill); ribbon (Offray); wooden letters (Michaels); acrylic paint (Plaid); tacky tape (Provo Craft); chalk ink (Clearsnap); glitter glue (Ranger); Mistral title font (Microsoft)

Index

Abstract photo collage 40

Accordion organizer 116

Additional supply lists 126

Altered box 108

Author tributes 120, 122

Backgrounds (custom) 14, 20, 84

Batik/resist technique 34

Bleeding (elements off page) 50

Board book (silhouette-cut) 104

Bulletin board 110

Burlap 18

Circular page 52

Clay board 32

Color risks 60

Cork 18

Cyanotype (sunprint) paper 22

Dichroic glass (faux) 36

Display album 98

Floam 28

Focal point
    changing the 56
    lack of 54

Hand stitching 24, 42

Hanging shelf 106

Inspiration 90

Introduction 6

Iron-on transfers 16, 118

Jewelry 112

Journaling
    lack of 58
    mixing up letters 64

Logos 56

Memory jars 100

Mixed metaphors 60

Molding paste & glazes background 20, 84

Optical illusion 46

Organic-shaped page 52

Outside the Album,
    Chapter Four 94-119

Paper piecing 30, 56, 114

Paper sculpture 114

Photography
    Digital photo effects 40, 42, 48
    Perspectives 62
    Photo surfaces 16, 18, 26, 32, 34
    Salvaging bad photos 42
    Telling a story through photos 88

Photojournalism 88

Playing with Techniques,
    Chapter One 8-37

Polymer clay 26

Rolled paper design 12

Scrapbooking
    to accept change 82
    to communicate feelings 80
    to document favorite items 86
    to document goals 68
    to educate 78
    to express gratitude 84
    as a healing tool 72
    the negative aspects of life 74
    as self-discovery 70
    to take time for yourself 92
    to uplift others 76

Scratch art 32

Silk-ribbon embroidery 24

Source guide 124

Stamping 14

The Motivation Behind,
    Chapter Three 66-93

There Are No Rules,
    Chapter Two 38-65

Tote bag (canvas) 118

Triptych mirror 102

Washboard wall art 96

Watercolor painting 14

White space 44

Wood burning tool 10

Woven paper 16

Discover More Ways to Stretch Your Artistic Imagination with Memory Makers Books!

What About the Words?

Journaling on your scrapbook layouts is easy with the advice, examples and inspirations found here.

- Paperback • 128 pages • Z0017
- ISBN-13: 978-1-892127-77-8 • ISBN-10: 1-892127-77-6

Imperfect Lives

Find page after page of inspiration and encouragement for capturing the "imperfect" slices of everyday life in scrapbooks.

- Paperback • 128 pages • Z0531
- ISBN-13: 978-1-892127-94-5 • ISBN-10: 1-892127-94-6

Focal Point

Discover unique and stunning ways to showcase your favorite photos with these fresh and fabulous altering and transfer techniques.

- Paperback • 128 pages • Z0530
- ISBN-13: 978-1-892127-96-9 • ISBN-10: 1-892127-96-2

These books and other fine Memory Makers titles are available at your local scrapbook or craft store, bookstore or from online suppliers, including **www.memorymakersmagazine.com**.